W9-CBU-225

Nicotine

Judy Monroe

—The Drug Library—

ENSLOW PUBLISHERS, INC.

44 Fadem Rd.   P.O. Box 38
Box 699   Aldershot
Springfield, N.J. 07081   Hants GU12 6BP
U.S.A.   U.K.

Library of Congress Cataloging-in-Publication Data

Monroe, Judy.
    Nicotine/Judy Monroe.
       p. cm.— (The Drug library)
    Includes bibliographical references and index.
    ISBN 0-89490-505-8
    1. Smoking—Juvenile literature. 2. Nicotine—Juvenile literature.
3. Tobacco—Juvenile literature. [1. Smoking. 2. Nicotine. 3. Tobacco habit.] I. Title.
II. Series.
RA1242.T6M59 1995
613.85—dc20   94-47280
                                                   CIP
                                                   AC

Printed in the United States of America

10 9 8 7 6 5 4 3 2

Illustration Credits: Anti-smoking Department, Minnesota Department of Public
Health, Minneapolis, MN, pp. 24, 37, 83; Clay H. Bartl, Illustrator, p. 18; Clay
H. Bartl, Photographer, pp. 48, 66; "© The Health Connection, 55 West Oak
Ridge Drive, Rockville, MD 21740." This poster is available from the Health
Connection, 1-800-548-8700, p. 50; National Cancer Institute, National
Institutes of Health, U.S. Department of Health and Human Services, p. 97;
Office on Smoking and Health, Centers for Disease Control and Prevention and
Health Promotion, U.S. Department of Health and Human Services, pp. 60, 77,
85, 102; Prints and Photographs Division, Library of Congress, pp. 9, 11, 13, 41.

Cover Photo: Daniel Hicks

Contents

1

History of the Golden Leaf

Because the earliest people did not keep written records, no one knows when tobacco was first discovered or how people learned to raise and use it. Since the 1600s, North America has been a major grower and supplier of tobacco. Today, tobacco is grown and used in many countries worldwide.

From the New World

Before the discovery of America, Native Americans grew and used tobacco in areas from southern Canada to southern Brazil. In 1492 when Christopher Columbus landed at San Salvador, he wanted to find gold. Instead, the Native Americans gave him tobacco. He thought it was worthless and threw it away.[1] He did notice, however, that many Native Americans smoked or chewed tobacco. Others sniffed it up into their nose through a tube. Spanish explorers and conquerors discovered another unpleasant use for tobacco during battles with Native South Americans. The Native Americans squirted tobacco juice into the Spaniards' eyes, which temporarily blinded them.

Spanish and Portuguese sailors and explorers adopted the use of tobacco. They brought their new addictions back to their homes and to other port cities they visited. Tobacco use soon spread across Europe and into other countries. By about 1575, every nation, including Japan and the Philippines, smoked or chewed tobacco, or used it as snuff.[2]

One reason tobacco use spread so quickly was that many people believed it could cure diseases.[3] European doctors and university professors wrote about the healing power of tobacco. In 1560 Jean Nicot, the French ambassador to Portugal, shipped tobacco to his queen for use in her herb garden. The word *nicotine*, which is the addictive drug found in tobacco, comes from Nicot's name.

Some people believed tobacco had magical or curative powers. For example, they used it to treat headaches, toothaches, asthma, stomachaches, lockjaw, heart diseases, and poisoning. "The smoke, it was said, was magnetic; especially effective when inhaled," one British writer explained. He thought it cleaned the lungs.[4] London pharmacies listed tobacco as a treatment for coughs.

In 1607 British settlers founded Jamestown, the first New World colony. The colonists barely survived in their harsh, new country. A turning point came in 1612, when the settlers planted tobacco seeds acquired from Spanish colonists in Trinidad and Caracas. Tobacco, known by the colonists as golden leaf, thrived in its new home. The first tobacco shipment sailed to England in

1613 and was eagerly snatched up. Londoners found the new tobacco superior to their own and demanded more.

Tobacco soon became the main export of North America. It was so important to the economy that colonists planted it in any cleared land—even in the streets! Tobacco often replaced money. Colonists used tobacco to pay for building churches or to pay ministers for marriages and burials. Some lonely Jamestown men bought wives with tobacco.

During this period, most farmers, including tobacco farmers, knew little about proper soil fertilization. Season after season, they grew their other crops in the same place until the plants removed too many nutrients from the soil. They then moved to new land and replanted. Once they exhausted that soil, many moved on again. The search for more farmland, along with the growing population, caused many colonists to move all along the Atlantic seaboard. Because of the rich soil and warm climate, farmers in the colonies of Virginia, Maryland, and the Carolinas grew the most tobacco. Later, people moved to Tennessee, Kentucky, Ohio, and further west, looking for more farmland.

Use of Snuff

Wealthy and important people, both men and women, made snuff fashionable by the 1700s. Snuffers did not need a tinder-box, candle, or hot coal to light snuff, so using it was safer and more readily available than smoking. People developed rituals around snuff—how to handle a snuff box, how to place snuff on a finger or nail, and how to inhale it. To keep their fingers clean, some women used tiny spoons to scoop out and inhale snuff.

Some suppliers advertised that their brand of snuff could

cure illnesses. One 1749 ad in London bragged, "I have published my Imperial Snuff for all disorders in the head; and I think I might have gone farther, and said, for all disorders of body and mind."[5]

The Rise of Cigarettes

By the mid-1800s, some tobacco shops in large cities carried and sold hand-rolled cigarettes to the carriage, or upper class, trade. Cigarettes were still hard to find, because each was rolled by hand, a slow process. Factories boasted that their fastest skilled rollers produced four cigarettes a minute.

After the Civil War ended in 1865, cigarette use increased. James A. Bonsack of Virginia helped this boom. In 1881, the twenty-two-year-old inventor received a patent for the world's first practical cigarette-making machine. By 1883, when it was first used in factories, his machine rolled up to 120,000 cigarettes a day. This rate equaled forty expert hand rollers working twelve and a half hours.[6]

Cigarette prices steadily dropped due partly to the faster cigarette-rolling machines. Many people could now afford a box of the cheap machine-rolled cigarettes. A typical box of ten cigarettes cost a nickel in the 1880s. By the 1890s, a box contained twenty cigarettes but still cost a nickel. By 1900, there were over one hundred sixty cigarette brands.

During the early 1900s, other tobacco products continued to be used in America, especially chewing tobacco and cigars. Cigarettes did not become the dominant tobacco product until the mid-1920s. In fact, they did not have a good image. Many people thought that cigarettes were improper and that only weaklings smoked them. One writer scoffed, "Who smokes 'em

Smoking tobacco—whether cigars, pipes, or cigarettes—had become a habit throughout the world by 1876.

[cigarettes]? Dudes and college stiffs—fellows who'd be wiped out by a single jab or a quick undercut. It isn't natural to smoke cigarettes. An American ought to smoke cigars . . ."[7]

By the early 1900s, cigarettes were favored by male teens, young adults, and immigrants. One-fourth of cigarette sales between 1895 and 1910 were made in New York City, the first home to thousands of immigrants. Men thought smoking was too masculine for women.[8] Strict laws existed for women who were caught smoking. In 1904, for example, a New York City policeman arrested a woman for smoking while driving.

Keeping Cigarettes from Teens

Along with the boom in cigarette use came a growing antismoking movement in the United States. Much of the movement focused on stopping teens from smoking because cigarettes "corrupted youth" or morally weakened young people.[9] But cigarettes appealed to teens.[10] Cigarettes seemed mild, although today we know that the nicotine in cigarettes is addictive. Cigarettes were also easy to use and could be hidden from parents. Cigarette manufacturers developed ways to market their products to teens. In 1878 trading cards and coupons were launched to increase sales. Smokers wanted to collect all the cards in different series.

Thomas Edison, Henry Ford, and other businessmen championed the antismoking movement. Henry Ford wrote a book called *The Case against the Little White Slave*. One famous antismoking leader was Lucy Page Gaston, a former schoolteacher. In 1899 she started the Chicago Anti-Cigarette League, which later became the Anti-Cigarette League of America. The League, with help from other similar groups and businessmen, helped push through many antismoking bills and

Since the early 1900s, adults have been concerned about keeping teens from smoking. These boys are feeling sick after smoking pipes and cigars.

laws. By 1890, twenty-six states restricted cigarette sales to minors. The age at which one could be considered a minor ranged from fourteen to twenty-four.

Some health concerns surfaced about cigarettes and heart disease, birth defects, and respiratory problems. Lucy Gaston's League said that twenty drugs, some poisonous, were in cigarettes. Few people listened to these warnings, not even many doctors. As late as 1948, the respected *Journal of the American Medical Association* reported that tobacco did not cause health problems and that smoking eased stress.

Cigarettes Take Off

The turning point for the growth of the cigarette industry occurred between 1913 and 1914, right before the United States entered World War I (1914–1918). According to Dr. John Slade, associate professor at the University of Medicine and Dentistry in New Jersey, cigarettes took off because a tobacco company used a large national mass media ad campaign to sell one of its cigarette brands. The company also sold the cigarette for less than other brands.[11]

World War I also helped the cigarette industry grow. After the United States entered the war, tobacco companies sent millions of free cigarettes to Americans fighting in France. Americans, both the troops and civilians, began smoking more. In 1910 less than ten billion cigarettes were produced. By 1919, the number had jumped to seventy billion.[12]

Cigarette smoking now became popular with both men and women, and the antismoking groups broke up. A strong lobbying effort from the industry was led by the Tobacco Merchants Association. By 1927 all laws banning cigarettes were

A smiling United States soldier in France during World War I has just received refreshments and cigarettes from the Red Cross.

reversed. World War II (1939–1945) helped the tobacco industry in another way. President Roosevelt declared tobacco an essential crop. This meant that tobacco growers did not have to fight in the war.

Today's Trends

Cigarettes continue to be the most popular form of tobacco worldwide. In 1993 the total cigarette output, including exports, was 670 billion pieces, and Americans smoked 485 billion cigarettes.[13] Use of smokeless tobacco is increasing, especially among teens. Tobacco products are easy to find and buy because most grocery and convenience stores sell them.

Many Americans, though, have raised concerns about tobacco use because of the enormous damage tobacco causes. Two trends have developed over the last thirty years. First, the antismoking or banning secondhand smoke movement, which started in the 1970s, has resurfaced. States and cities are again passing antismoking or clean air laws. Smokers are now often restricted from smoking in public places, or must smoke in special areas. Second, since the mid-1980s, a strong movement to stop and prevent tobacco use, including smokeless tobacco, has emerged.

Prevention, through education and treatment programs which help people deal with their addiction to nicotine, is becoming more common. Most schools now offer tobacco and drug education. Public awareness has increased about the many negative health effects of tobacco. Teens and adults are better informed so they can choose if they want to use tobacco—or how to quit, if they are current users.

Questions For Discussion

1. People probably began harvesting and using tobacco over five thousand years ago. Can you think of any foods or drinks that we still have today, that were discovered long ago?

2. Why do you think the early antismoking groups eventually failed?

3. Why do you think people believed tobacco products could cure diseases and illnesses?

2

The Effects of Tobacco and Nicotine

Most tobacco is stored for eighteen to twenty-four months prior to being turned into five types of tobacco products: pipe tobacco, cigars, cigarettes, snuff or dip, and chewing tobacco.

Today's Tobacco Products

Pipe tobacco is tobacco especially made and treated to smoke in pipes. Most pipe tobacco has added flavorings to enhance the taste. People who use pipes often smoke them for long periods of time. Depending on the blend, pipe smoke delivers nicotine to the membranes of the mouth or to the lungs.

Cigars are small rolls of tobacco leaf. Both costly handmade cigars and cheaper machine-made cigars have three parts: a filler, binder, and wrapper. The filler is the center of the cigar and is made of whole or chopped tobacco leaves. The binder wraps around the filler tobacco. A wrapper is formed around both the filler and binder. Cigars take about thirty minutes to smoke, and nicotine from cigar smoke is absorbed by the mouth.

Cigarettes are smaller than cigars and take five to seven minutes to smoke. Most are made of various types of tobacco leaves blended together, and manufacturers often mix in sugars, syrups, licorice, flavorings, and chemical additives. Cigarette paper is then wrapped around the tobacco. Most cigarettes sold today also contain filters at one end. However, according to Dr. John Slade, "Filters pretend to make cigarettes less hazardous, but cigarettes are dangerous with or without the filter. Nicotine from cigarettes is absorbed in the lungs. Cigarettes are designed to promote inhalation of the smoke."[1]

Growing Tobacco

Growing tobacco takes skill and hard work. About 136,000 farms in 23 American states, mostly in the South, and Puerto Rico, grow about 1.68 billion pounds or nearly 7 million tons of tobacco each year. The United States is the world's second leading tobacco producer.[2]

The world's largest tobacco-producing country is China. However, China is a land of many cigarette smokers—over 300 million. So, most of China's tobacco crop stays within the country.[3] Other countries that grow a lot of tobacco include India, Brazil, Turkey, the former Soviet Union, Zimbabwe, Greece, and Italy.

Tobacco plants thrive in warm, sunny climates. While the seedlings grow, farmers keep busy controlling weeds, insects, and plant diseases. The farmers use various chemicals to keep the tobacco plants healthy, including herbicides (for weeds), pesticides (for pests such as rodents), and insecticides (for

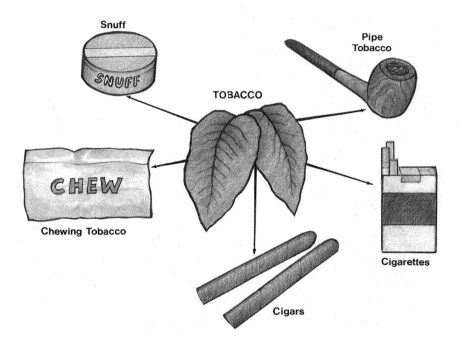

Snuff

SNUFF

Pipe Tobacco

TOBACCO

CHEW

Chewing Tobacco

Cigars

Cigarettes

The large tobacco leaves are processed into five different products.

insects). Some of these chemicals are absorbed by the tobacco plants. Although most harvesting is now done mechanically, many seasonal workers work the long, hot tobacco harvest.

Most tobacco in the United States is marketed through auctions. The U.S. Bureau of Alcohol, Tobacco, and Firearms (ATF) of the Treasury Department licenses and regulates tobacco processing plants. Machines in the cigarette factories churn out 9,000 sticks a minute.[4]

Tobacco: Economics and Death

Tobacco is a high value crop. This means that one acre of tobacco grosses several thousand dollars and the net grower returns are $1,000 to $1,500. The tobacco industry employs about seven hundred thousand people in the United States. However, whether tobacco is smoked, dipped, or chewed, its health effects are devastating. Each year, cigarette smoking causes 419,000 American deaths and $100 billion is spent on smoking-related health care costs.[5]

What's in Tobacco Smoke?

When people smoke tobacco, they take in over four thousand chemical compounds. Forty-three of these chemicals cause cancer. Cigarette smoke also contains radioactive chemicals. One researcher estimates that "an average smoker in one year absorbs radiation equal to that of 250 to 300 chest X-rays."[6] When smokers inhale tobacco smoke, they also breathe in small amounts of the chemicals used by farmers to keep their tobacco plants insect- and disease-free. Scientists do not know the health effects of these chemicals.

Harmful Ingredients in Tobacco Smoke

Nicotine   Highly poisonous, oily liquid that acts on the brain.

Tar   Thick, oily, dark mixture that causes cancers. It is not considered a chemical.

Carbon monoxide   Highly poisonous, odorless gas.

Ammonia   Colorless gas with an irritating odor used to make fertilizers. It is also used in household cleaners and explosives.

Butane   Gas used as a fuel and in lighters.

Hydrogen sulfide   Poisonous gas that smells like rotten eggs.

Acetylene   Colorless gas used as a fuel.

Benzene   Clear liquid used in cleaners, insect poisons, and fuels. It causes cancer.

Toluene   Colorless liquid used to make fuels, dyes, and explosives.

Arsenic, cyanide   Dangerous poisons.

Nitrosamines   Organic compounds, eight of which are found in tobacco smoke and cause cancer.

The three most health-damaging chemicals in tobacco smoke are nicotine, tar, and carbon monoxide.

Nicotine. Nicotine is a poison. Small amounts, ingested or injected, cause tremors (shaking), very slow breathing, nausea, vomiting, stomach pain, weakness, and headaches. A tiny amount—less than one drop—of pure nicotine can paralyze the nerves and slow the central nervous system of an adult man so quickly that he would die within a few minutes.

Nicotine in tobacco products acts as a stimulant. It speeds up a person's heart and central nervous system. The heart beats faster, blood vessels constrict or become smaller, and blood pressure increases. In turn, this decreases the amount of blood and oxygen that moves through a smoker's body.

Nicotine acts on the brain to produce addiction. Without addiction, tobacco products would not be attractive. Nicotine is the cause of continued tobacco use by any one person.

Nicotine also affects the brain and nervous system in other ways. Some smokers are calmer and more relaxed after smoking. Other smokers get more energy. Why the different effects occur depends on how much nicotine is inhaled and which brain cells it affects. Nicotine's effects come on quickly. Inhaled nicotine takes just seven seconds to reach the brain from the bloodstream. The average cigarette contains about 1.5 percent nicotine, or about six to eight milligrams of nicotine. The average cigar has about one hundred twenty milligrams of nicotine.[7]

Tar. When tar from tobacco smoke cools inside the lungs, it forms a dark brown or black sticky mass. Tobacco tar contains chemicals that cause cancers and lung diseases. Someone who smokes a pack of cigarettes a day for one year could inhale as much as four to eight ounces of tar.[8] That is the same weight as a stick of butter.

Carbon Monoxide. Carbon monoxide is a deadly gas released from burning tobacco and the exhausts of automobiles, trucks, and vans. When inhaled, it reduces the amount of oxygen in blood. Carbon monoxide levels in the blood of smokers are much higher than in nonsmokers. This means that they have less oxygen in their bodies. That is why most smokers often get short of breath or gasp for air when they run up stairs.

Health Hazards of Smoking

People who try smoking for the first few times usually get dizzy, light-headed, and nauseated. They cough and choke; some get quite sick. These reactions are typical, because their bodies are reacting to the poisonous and irritating chemicals in the smoke. If people continue to use tobacco, over time, the chemicals will affect their health.

The more people smoke, the greater their risk of developing tobacco-related diseases. The number of cigarettes smoked each day or the amount of tobacco smoked in a pipe is only one risk factor. Other factors are how many drags are taken and how large, how deeply the smoke is inhaled and held, and the level of nicotine and tar in the tobacco products.

Even one cigarette causes a smoker's heartbeat, blood pressure, and pulse to increase. Blood flow and air in the lungs change, and the temperature in fingers and toes decreases. The heart pumps less blood. Cilia inside the bronchial tubes also slow down. These tiny, hairlike structures move out dirt, bacteria, and mucus from a person's lungs. Mucus is a sticky, slippery material that protects the lungs. It takes twenty minutes after smoking one

22

cigarette for blood pressure, pulse rate, and body temperature to become normal. With continued smoking, the cilia disappear. But they can reappear when someone stops smoking.

Cancers

According to the National Cancer Institute, smoking causes about 30 percent of all cancer deaths. In 1993, about 149,000 people—or 93,000 men and 56,000 women—died of lung cancer in the United States.[9] Lung cancer is the number one American cancer killer for both men and women in the country. Smoking is responsible for 87 percent of all lung cancers reported in the United States.

Thousands of scientific studies have confirmed that using any tobacco product can cause cancers of the mouth, lip, tongue, and larynx (voice box). Smoking can also cause cancer of the esophagus (swallowing tube). Each year about eight thousand Americans die from oral cancers.[10] Smoking is a cause of cancer of the bladder, kidneys, stomach, cervix, and pancreas. The bottom line is that the more one smokes, the higher the risk of developing cancer.

Smoker's Cough

Smokers sometimes develop smokers' cough. This will usually occur early in the morning, when the smoker first wakes up. This happens because as smokers sleep, mucous that has collected overnight is in the bronchial tubes, ready to be cleared out. When smokers wake up, they cough because their lungs are trying to remove some of the harmful substances that built up from the previous day of smoking.

Smokers greatly increase their chances of developing all kinds of health problems.

Lung Diseases

Smoking causes chronic obstructive pulmonary (lung) disease (COPD) which is chronic bronchitis and emphysema. The term COPD is used because smokers can have both diseases at the same time. People with COPD have damaged and inefficient lungs and airways. Smoking tobacco causes most COPD, and about forty thousand smokers die from COPD each year.[11]

Here is what happens in COPD: When a smoker inhales tobacco smoke, the tar and gases irritate the lining of the airways and lungs. The gases slow down or paralyze the cilia, so that tar and more dirt stay in the lungs. This causes more mucus buildup. The extra mucus clogs the airways and interferes with normal breathing. This can develop into chronic bronchitis. Excess mucus in the airways causes smokers to cough a lot and have trouble moving air in and out of their lungs.

The irritation from tobacco smoke causes the air sacs' walls inside the lungs to dissolve and tear. Thousands of tiny air sacs line the lungs' surfaces and move oxygen from the lungs into the bloodstream. As air sacs dissolve, smokers get less oxygen from their lungs into their blood. As the lung surface area shrinks, people gasp for air to get more oxygen. At this point, emphysema, the most deadly COPD, can set in. This disease destroys the ability to breathe and can eventually kill. About two million Americans suffer from emphysema.

Mucus buildup in smokers' lungs also invites bacteria to grow. Smokers cannot fight off viral infections, such as flu, as well as nonsmokers. As a result, smokers develop more flu, pneumonia, coughs, tuberculosis, and other breathing problems compared to nonsmokers. An estimated 84,500 deaths from respiratory diseases such as pneumonia, influenza, bronchitis, and emphysema were attributable to smoking in 1990, according to the Centers for Disease Control. Smoking can also worsen the number and severity of asthma and allergy attacks.

Smoking and Heart Diseases

Smoking greatly increases the risk of major cardiovascular (heart and blood vessels) diseases (CVD). Heart disease is the number one cause of death in America. Approximately one hundred eighty thousand cardiovascular deaths were attributable to smoking in 1990, according to the Centers for Disease Control. Other factors that contribute to cardiovascular problems, such as a person's age, gender, and family medical history, cannot be changed. But reduced smoking or no smoking lowers the risk of disability and death from cardiovascular diseases. Low levels of cholesterol and blood pressure also help reduce CVD.

Hundreds of scientific studies have shown that smoking is a cause of heart disease. Smokers double their risk of dying from heart diseases compared to nonsmokers.[12] If smokers have either high blood pressure or high cholesterol their risk increases. If smokers have all three conditions, their risk jumps even higher. The risk also increases by starting to smoke at an early age, the number of cigarettes smoked each day, and how deeply smokers inhale.

Researchers calculate that smoking causes 30 percent of chronic heart disease deaths and 21 percent of other cardiovascular diseases in America.[13] If smokers survive a heart attack but continue to smoke, they are more likely than nonsmokers to have another heart attack. Pipe and cigar smokers have a slightly lower risk of developing heart diseases compared to cigarette smokers, but they still have a much greater risk than nonsmokers. Pipe and cigar smokers generally do not inhale as much or as deeply compared to cigarette smokers, so they inhale less tar and nicotine. However, people who switch from cigarettes to cigars or pipes have a much greater tendency to inhale.

Nicotine, carbon monoxide, and possibly other chemicals inhaled from smoking can cause arteriosclerosis, or narrowing of the arteries. These chemicals encourage fatty materials such as cholesterol to cling to artery walls. Over time, artery walls thicken and harden. Blood flow slows, so less oxygen travels to body tissues. This can lead to shortness of breath or even death from heart attacks or strokes.

Smoking also changes blood platelets. Blood platelets cause blood to clot. In smokers, platelets clot too fast and die too soon, which results in thickening of the blood. This can also lead to a heart attack.

Oral and Dental Health

Smokers may not notice, but others are often aware that smokers generally have bad breath and stained teeth. Tooth stains are especially severe in cigar smokers and tobacco chewers. Pipe smokers can develop uneven teeth from clenching the pipe stem, and their teeth tend to break more often. Gum diseases appear more often in smokers and in snuff users. This can lead to loose teeth, bleeding gums, and tooth loss.

AIDS

In 1993, a team of British researchers concluded from their study that, "If you have an HIV infection and you smoke, you are more likely to get full-blown AIDS." They think this happens because "of the effects that smoking has to the immune system," so that smokers have less resistance to disease.[14] HIV stands for human immunodeficiency virus. This virus usually turns into acquired immunodeficiency syndrome (AIDS), a disease with no cure.

When Mom Smokes, Baby Smokes

When pregnant women smoke, their babies are being forced to smoke, too. No one knows how many babies born to teens are harmed because the mother used tobacco while pregnant. Teen pregnancies are increasing in the United States. Today, teen mothers have more than 25 percent of all babies born each year. About 1.1 million teens get pregnant each year. That is about five teen girls out of every fifty. The number of teens under fifteen years old who get pregnant is rising. Eight out of ten of these teens say their pregnancies were not planned. This means that some teen smokers will continue to smoke because they do not realize they are pregnant, particularly in the early months of their pregnancy.

When a pregnant woman smokes, the various chemicals, including nicotine and carbon monoxide, also affect the baby. With dozens of poisons in cigarette smoke, it is likely that more than one can cause harm. When tested, these poisons are found in babies' saliva and urine. The more the mother smokes, the greater the amounts of these poisons are found in their babies.

One study found that mothers who smoked two packs a day lowered their blood flow to their babies. The developing babies had less oxygen, which could harm development. An unborn baby's organs, such as its heart and lungs, are immature and smaller in a pregnant woman who smokes. So the poisons from tobacco smoke probably stay in the baby's body longer than in the mother's.

Researchers now estimate that one out of ten fetal and infant deaths is caused by the mother smoking during pregnancy.[15] Babies born to women nonsmokers whose male partners smoke are more likely to be born too small. However, an even larger effect on birth weight comes from the mother's smoking.

If a teen or any woman smokes while pregnant, these problems could result:

- Her pregnancy could end in a miscarriage (natural premature end to pregnancy) or stillbirth (the baby is dead at birth).

- Her baby could be born too soon or too small. Babies born too small may have breathing and other health problems. Studies show that the more the woman smokes during pregnancy, the greater the reduction in birth weight.

- Her baby could die from Sudden Infant Death Syndrome (SIDS) or crib death. SIDS babies die without any warning. The Mayo Clinic estimates that infants are three times more likely to die from SIDS if the mother smokes during or after pregnancy.[16]

- Her baby could have learning and behavior problems. Many of these problems cannot be reversed.

- Her baby or child has a higher chance of developing leukemia, cancer of the blood.

Breastfeeding

Smoking makes it more difficult for women to breastfeed. Smoking lowers the volume of milk and the length of time a woman can breastfeed. The nicotine in cigarettes also seems to reduce the level of Vitamin C in breast milk.[17] According to a recent study from Baylor University College of Medicine in Houston, mothers who smoke produce somewhat less nutritious breast milk because it is lower in calories and fat.[18]

Other Health Problems

Two recent studies by Harvard University found that smoking may cause 20 percent of cataracts in the United States.[19] Cataracts turn the eye lens cloudy, causing partial or total blindness. Only a lens replacement operation can correct this problem.

Smokers develop more ulcers. If smokers continue to use tobacco, their ulcers are less likely to heal and more likely to kill them. People with diabetes further increase their risk for heart disease if they smoke. They are more likely to develop poor blood circulation in their hands and feet. This could lead to gangrene, or decay and loss of their hands and feet.

In 1993 the National Institute of Child Health and Human Development reported that women smokers are more likely to develop inflammation or swelling of the pelvis. This painful infection could result in the woman's infertility, which means that she could not have children. In the study, if a woman smoked more than ten cigarettes a day, she doubled her risk of getting pelvic inflammation.

Smoking also slows the healing of wounds, sores, burns, or surgery. Even a small burn from a hot skillet takes longer to heal if the person smokes. Smoking interferes with the body's ability to heal itself by constricting or tightening blood vessels, reducing oxygen in the blood, paralyzing the enzyme system that promotes wound healing, and damaging red blood cells. Smoking also increases the risk of infection after surgery and the length of time needed to recover after surgery.

Drug Interactions

Smoking and/or tobacco use may interact with many commonly used drugs. Doctors and pharmacists warn patients not to smoke if taking drugs, including some sold without a prescription, such as:

- Acetaminophen (commonly known as Tylenol®) which is taken for headaches and to reduce fevers.

- Antidepressants to treat depression.

- Caffeine—smokers generally do not react as strongly to caffeine as nonsmokers do.

- Vitamin B12—smoking lowers the level of this vitamin in the body.

Women who smoke and use birth control pills greatly increase their risk of heart attack or stroke. Drugs taken by smokers for diabetes, lung disease, and heart diseases may not work as well. Smokers may have to take more of these drugs to receive the same effects as a nonsmoker.

Safer Cigarettes?

Some smokers use lower tar and nicotine cigarettes in the mistaken belief that these lower their risks of developing tobacco-related diseases. However, researchers find that these smokers usually change *how* they smoke, so that they get the same amount of nicotine and tar as before. For example, they take more or deeper drags or smoke cigarettes to a shorter length. They often partially block the ventilating holes or channels in the cigarette filters. This cancels any small benefits of these products.

Menthol cigarettes are not safer than other kinds. Manufacturers add enough menthol, a local anesthetic, to create a sensation of coolness when smoking. People who smoke menthol cigarettes may inhale more deeply or hold the smoke inside longer compared to non-menthol cigarette smokers.

Addiction

Nicotine Is a Drug. In 1988 the Surgeon General of the United States published a report, *The Health Consequences of Smoking: Nicotine Addiction.* The Surgeon General is America's chief medical officer for health. The report concluded:

- Use of cigarettes and other tobacco products causes addiction.

- Nicotine is the drug in tobacco that causes addiction.

- Nicotine is addicting in exactly the same sense that heroin or cocaine is.

Tolerance to nicotine's effects begins with the first use. Tolerance is the process by which someone becomes used to nicotine so that the nicotine no longer has an effect at its original dose. The person now needs an increased amount of nicotine to get the same effect he or she used to get at a lower dose. So, repeated tobacco use leads to higher tolerance, which is why most smokers go from one or two cigarettes to a pack or more a day over a period of months to years. Eventually, tobacco users find a nicotine level that works for them. Tolerance seen in nicotine users is also seen among users of other drugs such as alcohol, cocaine, and heroin.

Most tobacco users are addicted to nicotine. An addict is dependent on, or controlled by, a drug. Nicotine is a drug because it affects the mood, feelings, and behavior of its users. Nicotine zooms to the brain in seven seconds and then peaks in the body at about the same time a cigarette is smoked to the butt, about seven to eight minutes. Within thirty minutes, most of the nicotine is cleaned from the blood. The need to use a drug regularly is another feature of addiction.

Most smokers eventually need at least ten cigarettes a day to keep some level of nicotine in their bodies. After a night's sleep, smokers often deeply inhale their first few cigarettes. This quickly raises the amount of nicotine in their blood. If someone is under a lot of stress and smokes more than usual, the person may become nauseated, dizzy, or get a headache.

Withdrawal

If deprived of nicotine, people who smoke regularly often experience withdrawal, or the process of the body becoming used to an absence of nicotine. People who stop using tobacco may have a craving for cigarettes, anxiety, increased appetite or craving for sweets, weight gain, mood changes such as irritability or anger, fatigue, difficulty concentrating, depression, headaches, and difficulty sleeping.

Questions For Discussion

1. Many heavy drinkers and alcoholics also smoke. This increases their chances of developing some types of cancer. Can you think of some of these cancer types?

2. What effect might nicotine have on teens' performance in sports and other physical activities such as bicycling?

3. Why do you think people who smoke and work with substances such as asbestos or coal dust have a greater chance of developing heart diseases?

Who Smokes?

Tobacco users come from every group in America. They include working men and women, retired people, and young people. They come from wealthy, middle class, and poor families. According to the latest National Household Survey on Drug Abuse, the largest number of smokers comes from low income families and people between the ages of twenty-five and forty-four. People with the least education are most likely to smoke. Smoking is most common in the southern part of the country, and least common in the West.

Smoking in America is becoming unpopular today, although forty-six million Americans—about 25 percent—still smoke. For the last twenty-five years, cigarette smoking has declined in all groups, except teens.

Children and Teens

For tobacco companies to continue sales at their current rates, they must replace the people who quit smoking or die. Tobacco companies recruit successfully, because each day, three thousand people start smoking regularly.[1] Tobacco companies focus their ads and promotions on young people for two reasons:

- There are huge earnings from this group—about $1 billion each year from tobacco sales to children and teens.[2] The American Heart Association estimated that in 1994, 2.4 million Americans aged twelve to seventeen smoked cigarettes. According to a 1994 study published in the *American Journal of Public Health*, teens spent about $962 million on 516 million packs of cigarettes in 1991.[3]

- Once young people have smoked more than a few cigarettes, most become addicted to the nicotine and remain steady tobacco customers for many years.

Today, young people begin to use tobacco at an early age. The average age of first time or experimental smokers ranges between eleven to fourteen years old.[4] The 1994 Surgeon General's *Report on Smoking and Health* found that 90 percent of adult daily smokers started before age eighteen; more than one-third start before the age of fourteen. This news is alarming, because the younger people are when they start smoking, the less likely they are to quit later. Studies show that the number of cigarettes teens smoke increases with age.

During the 1980s, smoking by young people remained at about the same level. That trend changed in the 1990s, reports Parents Resource Institute for Drug Education (PRIDE). This national organization surveys teen drug use, including tobacco, each year. This alarming trend was confirmed in a 1993

Children are smoking at earlier ages today, compared to twenty or thirty years ago, as shown by this anti-smoking poster which features a pre-teen.

University of Michigan survey of high school seniors. Since 1990, smoking by junior and senior high school teens has increased.

Why do teens start smoking? Some say they were curious. Others see their friends smoking and want to fit in. Still others say they are pressured or get offers.

Researchers find that the number one reason teens smoke is because of peer influence. If teens have friends who smoke, then they are much more likely to smoke. Jake Trippel agrees. "In my high school, kids smoke because their friends do. Smoking is an image thing, something that gives people confidence, especially among girls. In my senior high school class, about 80 percent of the girls and 40 percent of the guys smoke."[5]

Family influence is another big reason why teens smoke. Teens are much more likely—at least twice as often—to smoke if their parents smoke. Older brothers and sisters who smoke influence younger siblings, so that these teens are more likely to smoke. Family also influences in positive ways. The lowest levels of smoking are among teens whose parents do not smoke.

A lack of knowledge about tobacco contributes toward teen smoking. Most teens underestimate the power of nicotine addiction. They think that smoking for awhile does not harm them, and that they can quit after a year or two. In a survey of ten thousand teens, the National Center for Health Statistics found that smokers thought they would quit within a year, but three out of four could not.[6] In a study by the National Institute on Drug Abuse, nearly all the teen smokers said they would stop smoking within five years after leaving high school. But three out of four still smoked seven to nine years later.[7]

Cigarettes are easy to get. Parents who smoke usually have cigarettes at home. Remembers one ex-smoker, "I started sneaking around to smoke in junior high. My dad was a smoker at that time, so frequently a pack of cigarettes would be laying around and I would take a couple. I knew he wouldn't miss them."[8] When friends or older brothers or sisters smoke, they also keep cigarettes in easy-to-find places.

Although it is illegal to sell tobacco products to young people, store owners often do. Current laws are not always enforced. After analyzing nationwide studies, the Department of Health and Human Services Inspector General and the Americans for Nonsmokers' Rights, a national organization, concluded that teens can easily get cigarettes. Of young people who buy cigarettes, 84.5 percent bought cigarettes from small stores, 49.5 percent from large stores, and 14.5 percent from vending machines, according to a study in the *American Journal of Public Health*.

Researchers find common traits among teen smokers. Teen smokers generally do not join clubs or any other school activities. They tend not to play sports. Their grades are low and they do not like school. Teens with college plans smoke less than those with no plans for further education. One high school sophomore summed it up, "Only the losers smoke. They are the grubby kids who aren't into study or sports or school activities. They are the hangers around."[9]

Some teens say smoking offers benefits, that it relaxes them, keeps their weight down, or helps them cope with stress or other negative feelings. Some turn to smoking out of boredom or because they cannot get a job. At parties, if teens drink alcoholic beverages, they are more likely to smoke. However, the benefits do not add up when teens date. According to a survey for the American Lung Association, most male and female teens said they wanted to date nonsmokers.

As reported in the January 1993 issue of *The Nation's Health*, male and female teens are equally likely to smoke. Of all teens who smoke, white teens are almost twice as likely to smoke daily, compared to black teens. One in four Hispanic teens smokes daily. Of all sixteen- to eighteen-year-old teens who smoke, 20 percent smoke at least a pack a day.

"I think smoking leads to marijuana use," said one teen. "A 1993 survey in my school found that 15 percent of seniors use marijuana regularly because nicotine didn't give them a high any more."[10] According to the U.S. Surgeon General's 1994 *Report on Smoking and Health*, teen smokers are more likely to try and use alcohol, marijuana, and cocaine, carry weapons, and practice unsafe sex.

Women

Between 1974 and 1990, smoking among women decreased from 33 percent to 24 percent; smoking among men dropped from 43 percent to 28 percent. Yet this twenty-five-year decline in smoking may be ending. Between 1990 and 1991, smoking rates rose for the first time in many years due to increased smoking among African Americans and women.[11] This increase shows up in another statistic: lung cancer now causes more deaths for women than any other cancer, including breast cancer.

Why do women smoke? Nicotine, of course, addicts them and keeps them smoking. But many started smoking because of important people in their lives. Friends play a big part. Most teen smokers have at least one friend who smokes. Teen girls who smoke are more likely to have a best female friend or a boyfriend who smokes. If parents smoke, then their teens are more likely to smoke. Girls may also use cigarettes to avoid

By the mid-1920s, magazines began running ads like this to encourage woman to smoke.

weight gain; cope with tension or anger; or when they feel frustrated and powerless.

Researchers also say that cigarette advertising is a big influence. Some brands are aimed specifically at women. Ads display young, attractive, healthy, smiling models. Female smokers associate these false images with happy, slim, and successful women. Female smokers also say cigarettes relax them or that they use them as a reward after a meal or with coffee.

Female smokers risk several special health problems. They increase their chances of developing bladder cancer and cervical cancer. If women over age thirty-five use birth control pills and smoke, they create a much higher chance of having a heart attack or stroke. Smoking also causes loss of calcium and other minerals. The body needs these minerals to build and repair bones. When loss of calcium occurs, osteoporosis can set in. Osteoporosis, or brittle bone disease, affects 25 million Americans, usually women over age fifty.

Minority groups

African Americans. Over 7 million or about one-third of African Americans smoke today.[12] Far fewer black teens smoke compared to white teens. However, black adults are more likely than white adults to smoke. Fewer black adults quit smoking compared to white adults. And black adults are more susceptible to lung cancer from smoking than are white adults. These facts add up to much higher chance of lung cancer among black men compared to white men.

Cigarette companies target some brands to African Americans by advertising heavily in popular African-American newspapers and magazines. Billboards advertising cigarettes outnumber other types of billboards in city areas with high populations of African Americans.

Hispanic Americans. According to the Centers for Disease Control, about 21 percent of Hispanic Americans smoke. Billboards advertising cigarettes outnumber other types of billboards in city areas with high populations of Hispanic Americans.

Others. The American Lung Association estimates that smoking is highest among Native Americans and Alaskan natives; 39.4 percent of this population smoked in 1992. Asian Americans and Pacific Islanders smoke significantly lower than the national average, at 15.2 percent, according to the Centers for Disease Control.

Worldwide Smoking

To boost sales, tobacco companies sell cigarettes in other countries around the world, especially in Asia and Third World countries. Over the last twenty-five years, tobacco use worldwide has increased 70 percent. In the United States, cigarette exports have increased about 275 percent since 1985.[13] Each year, over 5.4 trillion cigarettes are made—that averages to over 1,000 cigarettes for each person in the world.[14] China, the largest producer of cigarettes, consumes one-third of the world's cigarettes.[15]

According to the World Health Organization, smoking causes 3 million deaths a year. If current trends continue, that rate could hit 7 million in Third World or developing countries within thirty years.

Governments in Canada, Australia, and Europe actively discourage smoking. Since 1980 Canada has raised tobacco taxes by nearly three dollars (U.S.) per pack and youth smoking has declined over 60 percent. In 1993, the Canadian government required stronger health warnings on cigarette packs, including "Smoking can kill you," "Cigarettes cause cancer," "Cigarettes cause stroke and heart disease," and "Cigarettes cause fatal lung disease." The government bans tobacco ads in newspapers and magazines, and recently banned tobacco billboard advertising.

In Australia, large warnings on cigarette packages are being proposed. The warnings, such as "Smoking causes lung cancer" or "Smoking Kills" will appear on the front of cigarette packages in large letters. The entire back cover will be covered with information about tobacco use and health risks, along with a "Quit Line" telephone number. The package sides will state the consequences of smoking and how much tar, nicotine, and carbon monoxide is in each cigarette. Canada, France, Hungary, Italy, Norway, and Poland ban all tobacco advertising. These and other European countries also restrict smoking in public places.

Other countries, though, have not followed these strong leads. American tobacco companies have aggressively advertised their products in Asian countries and Third World or developing countries. The results: the number of smokers in those countries has grown. In 1987 American cigarettes first appeared in Taiwan, along with magazine and newspaper ads. Now many more Taiwanese people smoke American cigarettes, and the overall rate of cigarette use in Taiwan has risen, especially among young people.

Japan leads the world in percentages of male smokers—61 percent of men and 14 percent of women smoke.[16] Japan bans selling tobacco to young people. However, just as in the United States, teens can easily find cigarettes.

In some Latin American and Caribbean cities, more than

half of the young people smoke.[17] Women in these countries are also smoking in increasing numbers. Most countries in Latin America and the Caribbean have some type of laws to restrict cigarette ads, and require smoke free places and health warnings on cigarette packages. The content of the laws and how well they are enforced varies between countries.

Puerto Rico, though, has taken tough no-smoking measures. Smoking is banned in restaurants, grocery stores, schools, theaters, and on public transportation.

While smoking is on the decline in America, it is growing at about 2 percent per year around the world. As many of us are becoming more healthy in the United States, the problem is getting worse in the developing countries.

Selling More Tobacco

Although the tobacco industry in America pays over $13 billion in taxes each year, tobacco is still one of the most profitable businesses in the United States. To increase sales, the tobacco industry promotes its products. Makers of tobacco products spend a lot of money on marketing studies to find the best ways to sell their products. Based on this research, the cigarette industry alone spends more than $4 billion a year on tobacco advertising and promotion.[18]

Tobacco advertising appears in magazines and newspapers and on shopping carts, billboards, subway trains, arena scoreboards, and buses. Advertising is based on imagery that falsely promises glamour, wealth, sex, and success from smoking or dipping. Some companies offer free cigarettes for mail-in coupons. Some tobacco companies have paid to have movie stars use their tobacco products on-screen. According to a recent

United Press International article, eight of the top ten movies in 1993 showed people smoking. The movie characters appeared glamorous and healthy when they smoked, because the movie directors rarely showed the real effects of smoking, such as coughing or clothing burns.

Athletes are often role models for teens and children, and sports magazines are avidly read by adults and teens. Some of these magazines include ads that indirectly associate tobacco with athletes. Athletes cannot endorse or promote cigarettes, but by running tobacco ads in the pages of sports magazines, publishers get readers to link sports with tobacco use. Sometimes sport calendars that promote specific cigarettes are included. Readers can easily pull out the calendars and hang them up. Some sports magazine covers have featured famous sports stars, smoking cigars and smiling.

Tobacco companies sponsor music and sporting events such as monster truck racing and car racing. These vehicles sometimes display large, colorful tobacco brand logos. These events attract both adults and young people. Some tobacco companies give away or sell T-shirts, posters, hats, and other items all decorated with cigarette logos. Several tobacco companies produce catalogs full of clothing and fun products that are free—except for the large number of empty cigarette packages required. These promotional items have no warning labels, and are popular with teens. They represent free advertising for tobacco products.

Advertising Ethics

Tobacco industry spokespeople claim their ads only encourage people who already smoke to try other brands. But every year, according to the national organization Stop Teenage Addiction to Tobacco (STAT), fewer than 10 percent of smokers switch brands. The tobacco industry has been questioned about the intent of their ads. Dr. Jean Kilbourne, former adviser to the U.S. Surgeon General, stated that the three main purposes of advertising are to get new users, increase use among current users, and influence users in their choice among competing brands. Antismoking ads are almost never supported by the tobacco industry.

Advertising and promotion create a myth. Tobacco ads and promotions tend to focus on themes that appeal to teens such as sex appeal, glamour, athletic ability, success, being popular, and keeping thin. Ads seldom educate or give information, except to misinform by creating a false sense of security or the idea that there is a relatively small risk associated with using tobacco products. Ads try to link a product with something people want. Since ads are so common, people tend to accept their messages. Tobacco ads try to promote use among nonusers and light users. They also appeal to the desires and fantasies of a target group that the industry wants to buy their products. Target groups include those under twenty-one years of age, women, and minority groups.

In 1994 Dr. Joycelyn Elders, former U.S. Surgeon General, published a comprehensive report on teens and smoking. She urged the Federal Trade Commission (FTC) to stop a tobacco company from using a cartoon character in their cigarette ads. Since the cartoon character first appeared, annual sales of this cigarette to teens has sharply increased. Other studies published in 1994 continue to show a link between teen smoking and advertising and promotion. One study's authors summed up their findings of teen smokers, "Tobacco advertising plays an important role in encouraging young people to begin this

Candy and gum that look like cigarettes are easily found and sell well in many stores.

lifelong addiction before they are old enough to fully appreciate its long-term health risks."[19]

Another trend about cigarette ads was recently uncovered. A 1992 study, "Cigarette Advertising and Magazine Coverage," reported that the more cigarette ads a magazine carried, the less likely it was to publish articles on the effects of smoking. This was especially true in women's magazines.

The FTC regulates advertising. It forbids unfair or deceptive advertising. However, it says nothing about tobacco advertising, other than banning the most blatant health claims in ads. The FTC regulates warning labels in cigarette and spit tobacco ads and on spit tobacco T-shirts, and other products. Congress bans all television and radio tobacco ads.

Tobacco companies self-regulate advertising. They say they follow their own code of advertising ethics. The Tobacco Institute, launched in 1958 by cigarette manufacturers, publishes a *Cigarette Advertising and Promotion Voluntary Code.* Updated in 1990, this industry code sets supposed standards for cigarette ads. However, there is no enforcement mechanism and no outside review. "The tobacco companies haven't lived up to their code and have backed off from following it, especially in recent years," said Diane Benjamin, ASSIST Field Director at the Minnesota Department of Health.[20] The ASSIST program focuses on reducing tobacco use in Minnesota.

Advertising Promotes Acceptance

Promotions, ads, television, and what goes on around them, teach young people that tobacco is part of everyday life. Studies find that cigarette sales increase when cigarettes are advertised. If

Smoking Makes You Look More Mature

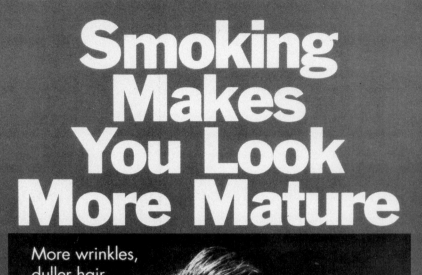

More wrinkles, duller hair, stained teeth— smoking really does make you look older.

Some people, including teens, do not realize that smoking can permanently affect their appearance.

tobacco advertising is banned, tobacco sales go down, especially with teen smokers.

In 1994 Dr. Joycelyn Elders published a report that analyzed forty years of tobacco studies. In the report, she concluded, "We shouldn't advertise something we know to be a poison and a killer," and called for a ban on tobacco ads.[21]

The Tobacco Institute runs a tobacco awareness program. In 1990 the Institute launched a large program to discourage youth smoking. One part is an educational program called "It's the Law," which encourages businesses that sell tobacco products to limit young people's access. The Institute produced a booklet for parents to help children deal with peer pressure. However, none of the Institute's materials mention that addiction, illness, and death caused by tobacco are the main reasons to avoid tobacco.

Inconsistent messages such as these pamphlets, along with the selling tactics of tobacco companies, create confusion about tobacco use. They send mixed messages to teens and adults. Tobacco manufacturers spend a lot of money on ads because tobacco advertising is effective. Ads and promotions encourage people, including children and teens, to start and continue using tobacco products.

Many magazines including *Reader's Digest*, *National Geographic*, *Good Housekeeping*, *Business Week*, *The New Yorker*, and *The Christian Science Monitor*, refuse to run tobacco ads. In mid-1993 the *Seattle Times*, the West Coast's largest newspaper, announced it would no longer carry cigarette ads.

Questions For Discussion

1. During Prohibition from 1919 to 1933, the sale of alcohol was outlawed in the United States. Nine states also outlawed cigarettes. All alcohol and cigarette laws were reversed. Based on these experiments, should the United States ban cigarette sales? Why or why not?

2. What are some of the ways the use of tobacco can detract from enjoyment of sports or typical activities such as bicycling or taking a dog for a walk?

3. How do you feel when you see adults smoking? What about if you see teens or children smoking? What do you think shaped your views?

Tobacco Use: A Dying Fashion

Tobacco quickly became an important cash crop for the New World colonists. They used it to buy and barter for Europe's manufactured products. Some European and American doctors believed that smoking cured many illnesses. They thought tobacco drained off mucus and that this helped people with tuberculosis, coughs, wheezing, and shortness of breath.[1]

The Rise of the Cigarette

With the first automatic cigarette-making machine in 1884, cigarettes started becoming more popular. Cigarette use got another boost from the invention of the match. Dr. Cooper, chair of the Virginia Interagency Council on Smoking Or Health, explained, "The invention of a safe, reliable, inexpensive match made it easy to light up anytime, and cigarette use soared as a result of the tobacco industry's practice of providing a free book of matches with each pack [sold]."[2]

Cigarette use climbed just before World War I. The increase continued due, in part, to the United States military. General John Pershing convinced Congress to issue cigarettes as part of a soldier's daily ration, starting in 1918. He said smoking made the soldiers tougher and better fighters. American soldiers received daily cigarettes up until the 1970s. This is no longer a common practice in the United States Military.

Many men became addicted to cigarettes and continued smoking after leaving the military. This changed Americans' views on cigarette smoking and by the 1920s, smoking cigarettes had become accepted. However, few women smoked before the 1920s. Rebels and leaders of some women's movements wanted the right to smoke, but men disagreed because they thought smoking was unladylike.[3]

The Cigarette Becomes King

After World War I, more women began smoking. Tobacco companies began promoting cigarettes to women. Magazine ads and fashion illustrations showed elegant women smoking cigarettes. By the mid-1920s, American women could smoke as freely as men.

During the 1920s and 1930s, American magazine and newspaper writers said that people had the right to smoke and that laws against smoking stepped on the personal freedom guaranteed under the United States Constitution. Some medical doctors endorsed smoking and said that tobacco did not cause health problems. With the collapse of antitobacco organizations, Americans became prosmoking. By 1930, all anticigarette laws in the United States were reversed.

The Health Link

In 1919 Dr. George Dock, chair of the Barnes Hospital in St. Louis, Missouri, and other hospital doctors closely watched a man dying from an unusual disease. After the man died, Dr. Dock asked his medical students to watch the autopsy. Because this disease was so rare, he said, his students would probably never see it again. The disease was lung cancer.

Two years later, a doctor at the University of Minnesota examined three men with lung cancer, all in one month. Since this was so unusual, he studied the University's medical records. He concluded that lung cancer was increasing. An English doctor reported in the *Lancet*, a respected medical magazine, that his patients with lung cancer also smoked. Scientists and doctors worldwide began publishing research that linked cigarette smoking with lung cancer. And by the late 1940s, medical reports began linking smoking and heart disease.

Cigarette companies began to emphasize supposed health benefits in advertising campaigns. Beginning in 1936, some national magazines ran full-page cigarette ads with health claims. Many quoted doctors who said that smoking cigarettes relieved tiredness, controlled weight, helped digest food, and protected against getting colds and coughs.

Golden Age of Cigarette Advertising

The growing health evidence against smoking did not curb Americans' tobacco use. In 1947 a hit song was "Smoke! Smoke! Smoke! (That Cigarette)." Families across America tuned in to their favorite radio shows; many were sponsored by tobacco companies. Throughout the shows, commercials aired with catchy tunes and slogans, urging people to smoke.

The early 1950s brought a new way for cigarette companies to advertise—television. Tobacco companies sponsored many TV shows and required the stars to smoke or have a burning cigarette in hand. In the 1950s many famous people supported smoking, including Humphrey Bogart, Ronald Reagan, Ed Sullivan, Nat King Cole, Lucille Ball, John Wayne, Bob Hope, and Bing Crosby. Today, of course, we are well aware of the many health dangers of smoking.

World War II boosted cigarette use. Soldiers still got cigarettes in their daily rations. If they wanted more, cigarette packs sold for five cents. When World War II ended in 1945, many soldiers brought their smoking habits home. Cigarette smoking continued to increase until the mid-1960s.

Changing Attitudes

In 1955 the Federal Trade Commission (FTC) banned tobacco companies from using health claims in cigarette ads. That same year, the National Cancer Institute, National Heart Institute, American Cancer Society, and American Heart Association began a combined study to determine if cigarette smoking caused lung cancer. Yes, said their report in 1959, but most Americans did not respond to this information. In 1965 Americans bought a whopping 529 billion cigarettes, an all-time high.[4]

In 1962 President John F. Kennedy told the U.S. Surgeon General to report on smoking and health. Surgeon General Luther Terry organized an exhaustive review of the scientific literature. Two years later, the Surgeon General's report stated that smoking caused lung cancer and other lung diseases. When people heard this, they reacted. Cigarette sales dropped. Congress, starting January 1, 1966, required a health warning on all cigarette packages.

Cigarette sales plunged as ads on television encouraged people to quit. The federal government continued to attack smoking. In 1970 Congress passed the Public Health Cigarette Smoking Act which made the smoking warning label stronger and banned cigarette advertising on radio and television. Unfortunately, this had the effect of removing the antismoking ads as well, and smoking rates increased.

In 1984 Congress wrote into law four alternative health warnings which are still used today on *all* packs of cigarettes:

- Cigarette Smoke Contains Carbon Monoxide

- Quitting Smoking Now Greatly Reduces Serious Risks to Your Health

- Smoking by Pregnant Women May Result in Fetal Injury, Premature Birth, and Low Birth Weight

- Smoking Causes Lung Cancer, Heart Disease, Emphysema, and May Complicate Pregnancy

There are no health warnings on pipe tobacco, cigars, or roll-your-own cigarette tobacco.

Problems Caused by Tobacco Use

Smoking is the leading cause of death in America today. It is America's number one public health problem.[5] Smoking causes more American deaths every year (419,000) than fires, automobile accidents, alcohol, cocaine, heroin, AIDS, and murders and suicides *combined* (247,000 deaths), which makes smoking the cause of one out of every five deaths.[6]

In 1993 according to the federal government's National Household Survey on Drug Abuse, fifty million or about 25 percent of Americans smoked cigarettes. Many smoked heavily (more than one pack a day). Heavy smokers run the greatest chance of developing tobacco-related diseases. Nationwide surveys show an increase in the number of teen smokers since the early 1990s.

Smoking costs Americans a lot. Each year, smoking adds up to $68 billion in health care costs and time lost from work.[7] Although great medical strides have been made in treating other cancers, 87 percent of people who develop lung cancer die within five years.[8] Most lung cancer deaths are due to smoking.

Fires started from cigarette smoking add up to much misery. Stan Stuart, Director of the National Fire Data Center in Emmitsburg, Maryland, stated that each year in the United States, 76,722 fires (38 percent of all fires) are started from cigarettes. Cigarettes are the most common cause of residential fire deaths, killing one hundred children each year. As a result of these fires, 1,220 people die, over 3,300 are injured, and property loss amounts to $400 million.[9] The Consumer Product Safety Commission (CPSC), based on major studies, has concluded that cigarettes can be manufactured to be less of a fire hazard.[10]

Tobacco Use Still Strong

Although 75 percent of adult Americans do not smoke, many do. Tobacco has been and continues to be a part of everyday life. Many people still think tobacco use is socially acceptable.[11] To-bacco products are easy to find. Many stores—1.5 million—sell tobacco products: tobacco shops, grocery stores, liquor stores, convenience stores, and drug stores. Cigarette vending machines sit in many businesses, restaurants, and bars. In the United States, cigarettes are cheap to buy.

Americans continue to give tobacco products a good image. Baseball players chew wads of tobacco then spit brown streams of tobacco juice before they "batter up!" When stars smoke on TV, they are shown as having a good time, and being successful and popular. A current study at the University of California in San Francisco found that smoking on TV shows is increasing and stars who smoke are shown as appealing, successful, and good-looking.

Some candy and gum products look like tobacco products. Children, teens, and adults can buy many kinds of tobacco-look-alike products, such as jerky chew, bubble gum chew and cigars, and candy cigarettes. Some new fathers proudly give pink or blue foil wrapped chocolate cigars to friends and coworkers. These products link fun and celebrations with tobacco products.

The Tobacco Business

Tobacco is a huge industry in the United States. Businesses want to make money and the tobacco industry increases its sales by getting new tobacco buyers and new markets. In 1993, according to The Tobacco Institute, Americans spent over $45 billion on tobacco products, mostly for cigarettes. Tobacco companies earned over $1 billion from tobacco sales to those under eighteen years of age. About 49,000 people are employed in tobacco manufacturing. Many thousands more are involved with tobacco sales, including transportation and advertising. This provides a large, powerful group with a strong interest in continuing and increasing the tobacco business.

Female smokers face special health problems. This poster suggests all kinds of ways for female teens to have fun without smoking.

Laws

Federal, state, and local governments in the United States set the laws regulating tobacco. For over twenty years, federal laws have required printed health warnings on cigarette packs. The warnings used in the United States are far weaker than those used in Canada or England. Warnings in the United States do not use the words *death* or *addiction*. The federal government also enforces regulations on tobacco manufacturing.

Federal, state, and local governments collect taxes on tobacco products. All states and the District of Columbia tax cigarettes; thirty-eight states tax cigars and smoking or chewing tobacco. States also restrict where smoking is permitted by passing clean air or public smoking laws. Most states limit smoking in public places, such as theaters, stores, public transportation, and in public workplaces. Some states restrict smoking in private workplaces.

States also restrict sales and use of tobacco products. Only people over age eighteen can buy these products. Age laws were set up to protect the health of young people. Children's lungs are still growing, and the substances in tobacco and tobacco smoke hurt their delicate tissues. Studies show that children who smoke are absent from school more often than nonsmokers because they get more colds, flu, and coughs.

State and local governments regulate the availability of tobacco. Since the 1980s, more and more states, counties, and cities have passed tobacco and smoking laws. Many counties and cities restrict or have removed cigarette vending machines and have banned smoking in restaurants, workplaces, or both.

Changing Attitudes: Healthy Lifestyles

Many Americans today are against tobacco use and follow healthy lifestyles. They know tobacco use impacts both health and appearance, although the effects differ for each person. Hair loses its shine, becomes dry and brittle, and smells like old tobacco smoke. Eyes can become red and bloodshot, with dark rings under them. Premature wrinkles can start even in teens because smoking ages the skin. Smoky breath might not be noticed by a smoker, but someone standing nearby can smell the musty, stale odor. Nothing, not even candy, mouthwash, toothpaste, or mints, wipes away tobacco-breath.

Smokers usually lose some sense of smell and taste. Spit tobacco users also lose some ability to taste. Colds generally last longer and painful sinus headaches are common. Other side effects include leg aches, cold toes and fingers, pale skin, yellow fingers, and white fingernails.

Smoking to control weight is a very bad trade-off. In exchange for a big risk of lung cancer, heart disease, and trouble breathing, a smoker keeps off an average of only six to eight pounds a year. Besides, a pack a day costs nearly $1,000 a year. Current studies show that weight gain, if any, is less than five pounds a year.

Many smokers and spit tobacco users smile with yellow or stained teeth. Dentists often cannot remove these tobacco stains. Tobacco users have more teeth and gum diseases and tend to lose their teeth early. Tobacco and smoke odors weave into clothing, hair, cars, and furniture, which makes smokers smell bad.

Questions For Discussion

1. If tobacco is taxed, do you think other things that can be harmful, such as fatty foods or candy, should also be taxed? Why or why not?

2. Since the United States government has said that secondhand smoke causes cancer, do you think cigarettes, pipe tobacco, and cigars should be made illegal? Why or why not?

3. Although tobacco and alcohol are legal for adults, alcoholic beverages are not sold in vending machines, but cigarettes are. Why do you think this difference exists? Should cigarette vending machines be removed? Why or why not?

5

Families and Smoking

Studies show that smoking tends to run in families. Why this trend exists has fueled debates among researchers. Current research suggests that both genetics and the environment, or the homelife, are factors.

Genetics

Little is known about the role of genetics, or heredity, in people's smoking habits. The few published studies report a small positive effect. For example, a 1993 study found that for smokers aged thirty-one or older, genetics is a factor in whether these people continued to smoke.[1] Other studies indicate that some people tend to become smokers because of their genes. This means they may be predisposed to smoking.

Recently, the SRI International Institute in California studied four thousand male twins. The researchers concluded that genes may influence whether someone starts smoking and how many cigarettes are smoked (i.e., heavy or light smoker). Genes may also indicate whether someone will smoke at all.

Another researcher examined all genetics and people's smoking habits studies up through 1990. The family and twin studies he studied showed that both genetics and the environment help determine when a person starts smoking, how much he or she will smoke, and if he or she will continue.

The Environment

Some scientists say that the family is the main influence on tobacco use by teens. One woman remembered that, "It was understood in my family that I'd be a smoker. They were all smokers: parents, aunts and uncles, grandparents, and even my two older sisters. My dad requested that I not smoke until the age of eighteen, so I dutifully lied about it and hid my smoking. Then on my eighteenth birthday, I was given a carton of cigarettes as a present. It was my passage to adulthood."[2]

Parent examples are a powerful influence on teens. Parents are role models for adult behaviors, and children and teens often imitate what they see their parents do. So, if parents smoke, studies show that their teens are ten times more likely to smoke.[3] Smokers' children grow up with the idea that smoking is all right. Parents who smoke often have friends who smoke, which reinforces the idea that smoking is the norm. However, if parents smoke, some teens decide not to smoke because they see tobacco's consequences: yellow fingers, stained teeth, bad breath, and clothing and a home that reeks of stale tobacco smoke.

Researchers find that the family is very important in helping children, preteens, and teens say "No" to smoking. The greatest

If parents follow a healthy lifestyle, including regular exercise and a no-smoking policy, then their children are much less likely to smoke.

risk for starting to smoke comes in preteen and early teen years. Research shows that the earlier young people begin to use tobacco, the more likely that they will continue to use it and have a harder time quitting.

During grades seven to nine, peer influence is the main factor in whether teens start smoking. If teens smoke, they generally start before leaving the ninth grade. Although some teens push away their parents and lean more heavily on friends, researchers find that parents are still very important as role models. Positive parent role models, such as following a healthy lifestyle, impact more on teens than lectures about "Tobacco can kill you." If parents talk about tobacco use and appearances, such as stained fingers and teeth, bad breath, and burnt clothing, while not using tobacco themselves, teens are also more likely to listen and absorb this information. Researchers agree that parents must be clear about their rules and expectations.

By the time teens reach senior high school, they still continue to be influenced by their friends. However, older teens think more about their future and may turn to their parents for ideas and discussion. Parents continue to be role models for nontobacco use. Parents can also stress the importance of older teens serving as role models for younger brothers or sisters.

Nicotine Is an Addiction

Studies show that parents, whether smokers or nonsmokers, want their teens to avoid tobacco. Some teens try smoking once or twice, but never continue. Other teens who start smoking continue and become addicted to the nicotine. Most teen smokers do not believe they will become addicted and that they can stop at any time.[4] However, this is incorrect. If smoking continues, addiction usually develops.

Parents, say researchers, need to explain the nicotine addiction that occurs with all types of tobacco products, including cigarettes and smokeless tobacco. Most smokers take in a steady amount of nicotine all day long, every day. A pack-a-day smoker gets more than seventy thousand nicotine drags or hits in one year. This is more drug hits a year compared to any other drug used.[5]

Because nicotine is a powerful drug, tobacco users often go through great discomfort when trying to quit. If parents smoked, but quit or are trying to quit, they can explain to their teens why quitting is hard and they can talk about some of the problems they have had.

Addictive Personalities?

Science cannot yet say what causes people to become addicted to nicotine. Some researchers are investigating what makes up an addictive personality. They want to know if drug users have traits in common and if some people are naturally prone to drug abuse, including nicotine.

Parents Who Are Addicts

Researchers find that parents who are addicts—whether the addiction is to tobacco, alcohol, or illegal drugs—often raise teens who have a tendency to become addicts. That is because children and teens absorb what their parents do and then tend to repeat those same behaviors. Signs of addictive parents include:

- *Inconsistent parenting.* Addictive parents tend to give too much or too little discipline, love, and expectations. These parents flip between extremes and their teens learn to become wary and untrusting. Teens do not know what to expect.

- *Low pain tolerance.* When they do not feel well or are upset, addictive parents tend to turn to drugs to get rid of the pain. The drugs may be prescribed by a doctor or bought over-the-counter, such as aspirin. Addictive parents look for easy ways to handle pain, whether the pain is physical or emotional.

- *Poor problem-solving skills.* When problems occur, addictive parents often do not know how to handle them. Instead, they turn to easy substitutes such as smoking or using other drugs, watching TV, going shopping, or buying more lottery tickets. Teens learn not to discuss problems and to hide their fears and concerns. They also do not get parental examples of how to solve real-life problems.

- Low self-esteem. Parents who lack confidence or hope convey those beliefs to their teens.

Signs of Tobacco Addiction

If parents ask their teen smokers if they are addicted, most would say "No." Most teens would probably say, "That can't happen to me," because they feel invulnerable or that nothing bad will happen to them.[6]

The Smoking Education Program of the National Heart, Lung, and Blood Institute lists nine signs of an addicted smoker:

- Smokes within thirty minutes of waking up.

- Enjoys the first cigarette of the day the most.

- Smokes more in the first two hours after waking up.

- Smokes in the middle of the night if he or she wakes up and has trouble going back to sleep.

- Inhales the smoke.

- Finds it hard not to smoke in smoke-free situations.

- Smokes when he or she is ill enough to stay in bed.

- Smokes more than twenty-five cigarettes a day.

- Smokes a high-nicotine brand[7].

While you may have one or more of these signs, you may not be addicted. You might also want to see if you are addicted by not using tobacco for a day or two. If you have withdrawal symptoms, then you may be addicted.

Parents Can Help Teen Tobacco Users

Researchers find that parents can help teens with their nicotine addiction. The most important thing parents can do is quit smoking, if they currently smoke or use spit tobacco. Teens generally will not take their parents' tobacco rules and expectations seriously if their parents smoke.[8]

Many parents who smoke must also learn new attitudes if they want to break their addiction. According to a 1993 study in the *American Journal of Public Health*, researchers found that many more smokers, compared to ex-smokers or nonsmokers, believe tobacco myths, such as:

- Most people smoke.
- Many smokers live a long life, so cigarettes are not all bad.
- Most lung cancer is caused by air pollution.
- If you have smoked for years, it is too late to quit.[9]

Some parents pretend that their teens are not using tobacco. Their teens probably will not tell them if they are. Concerned parents can notice if their teens smell like smoke, their money disappears fast, and they leave matches and lighters in their pockets. Teens who use tobacco tend to leave the house or disappear at odd times, so they can smoke, dip, or chew without their parents' knowledge.

Parents, researchers agree, should confront their teens. If their teens are smoking, parents can talk with and listen to their teens. One rule must stay, though: all tobacco use must end. If parents smoke, the parents and teens can agree to a pact in which everyone must quit. If teens cannot stop smoking, parents can help them find a quit-smoking program.

Questions For Discussion

1. Sometimes it is hard for teens to ask for help. Suggest some ways teens can ask for help.

2. Do you think all tobacco products should be banned? Why or why not?

3. How would you suggest a teen who does not use tobacco deal with parents who smoke or with siblings who smoke?

6

How to Quit and Prevention

Each year, more than three million Americans quit smoking, according to the National Institutes of Health.[1] Three out of four smokers say they want to quit, while seven out of ten smokers have tried to quit smoking.

David Bresnick knows how powerful nicotine addiction is. He developed throat cancer from smoking cigarettes and one night, he remembered that, "I was walking home, coughing up more mucus and phlegm than usual. I decided I'd had it. So I crumbled up my pack of cigarettes and threw them in an alley near my home. At three in the morning, I was in the alley on my hands and knees with a flashlight, searching for that pack of cigarettes."[2]

What does it take to quit? Researchers agree: strong motivation, consistently following a plan, support of family and friends, and for some people, help such as smoking cessation programs. The most important factor is to keep trying. People

73

rarely quit for good the first time they try. Many types of treatment exist for people of all ages who want to quit using tobacco. No one treatment works for everyone, but the first step is deciding to quit.

Deciding to Quit – Who Quits?

Most smokers want to quit. Polls show that between two-thirds and three-quarters of smokers say they would like to quit.[3] Quitting can be hard, though. Out of every one hundred smokers who try to quit for the first time, fewer than twenty succeed.[4] Most ex-smokers tried to quit at least once or twice before succeeding. Some people require three, four, five, or more tries before they finally quit.

The number one reason teens stop smoking, researchers report, is because of cost. A high school senior agreed, "I've never known one kid who quit because of the threat of cancer or other health problems from using tobacco. Everyone's heard that stuff in school. The reason kids quit is because it costs too much."[5] The 1994 U.S. Surgeon General's *Report on Smoking and Health* calculated that a teen could play twenty-eight hundred arcade games with the savings from quitting for one year.

Other people want to quit to feel in control again, as explained by this young woman. "I'm twenty-one, and have been smoking since I was nine. I hate smoking. I hate running out at all times to buy cigarettes. I hate the smell, I hate the burns, and most of all I hate the power cigarettes have over me."[6]

Benefits of Quitting

According to the U.S. Surgeon General, quitting carries big health benefits for men and women of all ages, including older

Reasons for Quitting

The reasons why people quit vary:

- Improved health.

- Better breathing, cough less, walk without running out of breath.

- Less colds and flu.

- More energy.

- Better blood flow, fingers look normal.

- Decreased risk of developing heart and lung diseases.

- Improved taste and smell.

- Better sleep.

- Helps eliminate insomnia caused by nicotine.

- To protect loved ones.

- No longer harming family and friends with secondhand smoke.

- Parents and grandparents want to live longer for their children.

- To be a role model for children and grandchildren.

- For improved acceptance.

- Today, most people do not smoke and are bothered by it when people near them do.

- Workplace is smoke-free, so they cannot smoke there.

- To save about $1,000 for one year at one pack a day.

people. Ex-smokers live longer than those who continue to smoke. Quitting also decreases the risk of cancers, heart disease, stroke, and chronic lung diseases. After one to two years of not smoking, the ex-smoker's risk of a heart attack drops sharply and gradually returns to normal after about ten years. Other health effects are even more immediate: less chest discomfort and coughing, easier breathing, and having more energy and a better sense of taste and smell.

By quitting, you protect your family and friends. Family members of smokers are more likely to get lung problems, especially children who get sick more often with colds, flu, ear infections, allergies, and lung diseases. You are also a role model for your family and friends.

When you stop smoking, your clothes and hair do not smell anymore. Your car, closet, and school locker do not reek of smoking fumes. Smoke doesn't stick to the windows, walls, and wallpaper. And you save money, at least $1,000 a year if you smoked a pack of cigarettes a day.

Ways to Quit

People use a variety of methods to quit smoking. Some smokers can quit on the first try, but others need to try combinations of methods before finally succeeding in quitting. Here are some popular methods.

Self-instruction is the most successful way to quit. Researchers find that most ex-smokers quit on their own. Self-instruction approaches include booklets, books, videotapes, and quit kits. The National Cancer Institute, American Cancer Society, American Heart Association, American Lung Association, and other organizations offer a variety of quit

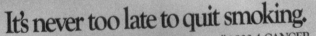

People of any age can benefit from quitting smoking.

smoking publications. People use these materials because they are flexible, private, and do not cost much. These materials help people determine their smoking patterns, set a date for quitting, think of alternatives to smoking, limit any weight gain, and learn to relax and reduce stress. Most materials offer suggestion on handling slips.

Most people first try quitting "cold turkey." They decide to quit, pick a date, then quit. They often throw away cigarettes, lighters, and ash trays and vow to never light up again. Follow through requires some practice, determination, and consistent behavior.

Some people use over-the-counter aids, such as special cigarette filters or smokeless cigarettes. Brand switching is another step-by-step approach to quitting. Current research finds that tapering off works well because the body gradually adjusts to the decreasing amounts of nicotine. This makes nicotine withdrawal, especially nicotine cravings, less painful. People also gradually learn how to cope without cigarettes. However, tapering off is hard to do without professional help, and you must clearly set a quit date, then stick to it.

Nicotine chewing gum and the nicotine patch are powerful ways to deal with nicotine withdrawal. However, they are not magic. For teens, these should be used only if they find it hard to quit. Nicotine chewing gum helps people stop smoking right away. Nicotine replacement therapy is only used when all smoking has stopped—on quit day and beyond. Doctors or dentists must prescribe nicotine gum and instruct—and have you practice—on how to use the gum properly. To begin, people stop smoking and instead chew ten to fifteen pieces of gum each day. Each piece releases small amounts of nicotine. Over time, people chew less and less gum. Nicotine gum is not designed to be used alone; it should be combined with quit-smoking programs. Do not smoke while using nicotine gum. Smoking while using nicotine gum could result in an overdose of nicotine.

First used in 1991, nicotine patches help people quit when used with a quit-smoking program. Doctors must prescribe the nicotine patch, which is a small pad that contains a gel. When the patch is placed on the arm, chest, or back, the nicotine inside the gel slowly passes through the skin and into the bloodstream. Twenty-four hours later, when all the nicotine is gone, smokers remove the patch and put on a new one. The quitting process with nicotine patches takes six to eight weeks.

While 90 percent of former smokers quit on their own, some people need or want the support of group programs to quit smoking. Members must commit to regularly scheduled meeting times. Program costs and success rates vary. One successful group program is the American Lung Association's "Freedom from Smoking." Pam Solstad has been a facilitator and group leader for this program for four years. She quit smoking eleven years ago. "It's fun working with people and exciting to see them quit and stay with their decision." Her group members respond well; 60 percent or more stay off of cigarettes for at least two years.

"The groups are motivated, but skeptical at the start," she continued. "The first night I ask everyone to explain why they want to quit. Reasons vary, but most say it's for health, kids, or family. Some feel like social outcasts because most of their friends don't smoke. Many companies don't allow employees to smoke at work, so they smoke outside. This is Minnesota we're talking about, and it gets very cold. It's no fun freezing at 20° below zero, puffing on a cigarette!"

Pam Solstad finds that most group members have tried to quit three to five times before. "People smoke as a stress reliever. They are addicted to the nicotine, but also it's been a habit. Most started as teens, at thirteen, fourteen, or fifteen years old, because of peer pressure.

"Most members are women, but more men have been attending. Ages vary, but usually people are in their fifties and sixties. My current group is of people in their thirties and forties. My oldest participant was seventy-four years old. He started at age thirteen and smoked heavily since, nearly two packs a day. He did quit! My youngest was thirteen years old. He was caught smoking at school and was forced to go to this program. He didn't quit. Only people who are ready to quit will quit. They'll find whatever way works for them."[7]

People who are heavily addicted to nicotine may find live-in programs offered by some hospitals and clinics helpful. In these programs, people live there for several days to a week and go through many quit-smoking activities. This can include group support and counseling, changing smoking behaviors, exercise, diet changes, and education about health risks from smoking. These programs are costly. Due to the fact that most participants are among the most heavily addicted to nicotine, their success rates vary.

Other Methods Not Medically Proven

Other ways of quitting smoking are not medically proven. Hypnosis helps smokers focus on smoking patterns, then change their attitudes about smoking. While hypnotized, smokers receive suggestions from licensed therapists, such as to relax if the urge to smoke strikes, or to feel good if they pass up a cigarette. For some people, these suggestions stay in their minds after the session ends and they avoid smoking. William Hoffman, executive vice president of the American Society of Clinical Hypnosis, stated that hypnosis "won't make you stop smoking, though it's a very supportive and helpful tool."[8]

Acupuncture has a low success rate for helping people quit smoking. In acupuncture, small needles or staples are inserted into the skin near specific nerve endings. These nerve endings, say the therapists, are connected to organs and functions in the body. To end smoking, therapists pinpoint specific places on the ears, nose, and wrists.

Conditioning methods or aversion therapy try to change smoking behaviors. In conditioning, instead of reaching for a cigarette, people drink water or take a short walk, for example. In aversion therapy, people smoke so many cigarettes at regular intervals that they get nausea, headaches, and foul breath. By associating cigarettes with these negative reactions, some people quit. Both methods are sometimes used in quit-smoking programs.

Relapses

Most people who quit relapse or have at least a brief period where they start to smoke again. Pam Solstad explained, "Relapses usually occur because of a crisis. An ex-smoker suddenly has to deal with something big and without thinking, out comes a cigarette. The other main reason is because they're in a situation where others are smoking. Bars, parties, card games—those are dangerous times because ex-smokers think they have control and can smoke one cigarette. Before they know it, they're smoking again."[9]

One thing that researchers find that helps ward off possible relapses is preparation. Pam Solstad agrees, "Take quitting in increments—it's the best way. If people make it through days one through three, the hardest days of withdrawal, they stand a good chance of quitting. If they make it through the withdrawal period, which usually lasts three weeks, they stand an even better chance of quitting. And if they can last three months, six months, nine months, and up to a year, they'll be ex-smokers."[10]

The best way to deal with a relapse is to take a one-day-at-a-time approach. If a slip occurs, get back on track right away. With consistent effort, most who keep trying eventually will stop smoking for life.

Prevention

In the United States, prevention methods work to reduce the number of people who smoke as well as to stop people from ever starting. No one prevention method reaches all people. Today, the federal government, health professionals, teachers, business people, parents, teens, and many other people are all involved in various prevention methods.

Prevention in the United States is a network of complementary strategies and tactics. Control of secondhand smoke, or pollution control, is one strategy. Some other strategies include increasing tobacco product prices, decreasing availability of cigarettes, decreasing the marketing of tobacco products and promotions, and counter-marketing by antismoking organizations and people.

School Programs

Schools set smoke-free examples. Campuses must be smoke-free for students, staff, and visitors. Without this policy, all else is a

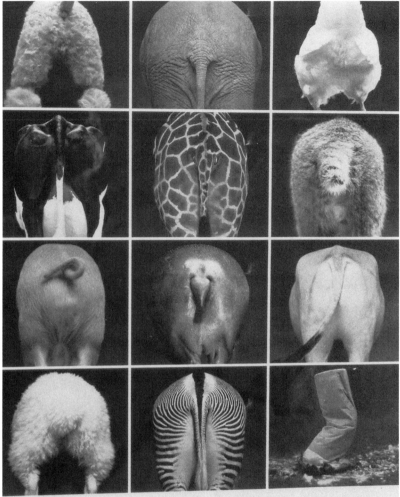

Butts Are Gross.

Encouraged by the strong antismoking stand that has swept across America, smokers can turn to a variety of antismoking programs and materials to help them quit.

double message. Most schools offer drug education programs for elementary, junior, and senior high school students. Some schools, such as those in California, are required to teach students about nicotine. These schools must show a decrease in smoking by students. Some schools target young children, including first- and second-grade students. They inform students about nicotine and other drugs, and help them develop good problem-solving skills and build self-esteem. Researchers find that when children go through these programs, they are less likely to start using products that contain nicotine.

The Office for Substance Abuse Prevention in the federal government's Alcohol, Drug Abuse, and Mental Health Administration has a multiyear public education program, "Be Smart! Don't Start!" It teaches teens about tobacco, alcohol, and other drugs.

One highly praised prevention program that focuses on preschool children through senior high school students is Beginning Alcohol and Addiction Basic Education Studies (BABES). BABES was founded in 1979 by Dr. Lottie Jones in Detroit, Michigan. It is used in every U.S. state and five other countries including Russia. It can be used in schools, churches, and child care centers.

The program helps children and teens learn and practice living skills to make positive early decisions about the use of drugs, including nicotine. For young children, BABES materials include colorful puppets, real-life stories, flash cards, worksheets, and cassettes and videotapes. Videotape number eleven is "Learning about Smoking: Does It Really Make You Cool?" The materials change a little for teens, but the information is the

THE PERFORMANCE EDGE

TOBACCO AND ALCOHOL DON'T MIX WITH

Some teens do not realize that combining smoking and drinking decreases their ability to do well in activities that require skill, quick reflexes, and good judgment.

same, such as self-image and feelings, decision-making and peer pressure, and coping skills.

Schoolteachers also teach students about staying away from nicotine. Andrew Dixon of Rancho High School, North Las Vegas, Nevada, said, "Our head baseball coach, who also teaches health courses, has shown his players the effects of smokeless tobacco. He won't allow us to use it on the playing field, and encourages us to not participate in the use of smokeless tobacco off the field. I believe that he has a great effect on all of his players."[11]

Federal Government

Two federal agencies are largely responsible for directing the U.S. Government's tobacco and health policies: the Environmental Protection Agency (EPA) and the Occupational Safety and Health Administration (OSHA). The EPA and OSHA work closely with the World Health Organization. Anyone can contact the EPA or OSHA for information on smoking prevention, smokeless tobacco, health effects, and quitting. The U.S. Surgeon General issues regular warnings about the dangers of nicotine addiction.

The government also has a powerful way to reduce the number of people who use tobacco: raising tobacco taxes. Federal, state, and local governments set various taxes on tobacco products. In late 1993 Dr. Samuel Broder, director of the National Cancer Institute, published a report that said a large tax on cigarettes was probably the best way to quickly reduce smoking among all age groups. If tobacco product taxes were increased, it is likely that more teens and Americans with low incomes—who have the highest smoking rates—would quit.

Secondhand Smoke

In December 1992 the EPA classified secondhand smoke as a Group A carcinogen, known to cause cancer in humans. Secondhand smoke is what nonsmokers breathe in as someone else smokes. Billions of dollars are spent to remove asbestos, another Group A carcinogen, from public places. Tobacco smoke can be eliminated in public places by laws. Federal bills for smoke-free public places are now being proposed. The Occupational Safety and Health Administration has proposed a ban on smoking in most workplaces.

The Synar Amendment, a federal law passed in 1992 as a part of the Alcohol, Drug Abuse, and Mental Health Administration Reorganization Act, requires states to enforce laws that prohibit sales of tobacco products to minors. The law went into effect on October 1, 1993.

Organizations

Various groups in the United States work to prevent tobacco-related death and illness. These pro-health advocacy groups often combine their efforts. Among their activities, they help communities limit the availability of tobacco products, fight against tobacco advertising, and educate people with current, reliable health information about tobacco.

The World Health Organization (WHO) sponsors its annual World No-Tobacco Day each spring. This event helps draw attention to tobacco issues as part of a worldwide problem. The American Cancer Society (ACS) promotes a national smoking control movement. The ACS, American Heart Association, and American Lung Association (ALA) offer information and education programs on tobacco and secondhand smoke. Both the ACS and ALA run stop-smoking programs.

Since 1977 the ACS has sponsored its annual Great American Smokeout. The Smokeout's goal is to show smokers they can quit for a day. In 1993 this one day saved American smokers $17.8 million, because 9.7 million packs of cigarettes were not smoked.

Stop Teenage Addiction to Tobacco (STAT) is a national tobacco control organization founded in 1985. It is the only national organization specifically geared to young people. Its members come from all fifty states and all over the world. Headquartered in Springfield, Massachusetts, STAT's goals are to decrease and prevent tobacco addiction by young people, decrease and eliminate sales of tobacco products to young people, and expose and decrease the influence of unethical tobacco company advertising directed at young people. STAT members are involved in community projects, public education and information, and research. They publish a quarterly newspaper and write magazine and newspaper articles and radio and video ads. They also provide an Adult/Youth Speakers Bureau and train teens to counsel other teens.

Action on Smoking and Health (ASH) is a national organization concerned with the problems of smoking and nonsmokers' rights. Founded in 1967, ASH focuses on nonsmoking laws and policies to protect nonsmokers' rights. ASH is concerned with the negative effects of smoking, unfair and deceptive cigarette advertising and promotion, and making the tobacco industry pay for harm caused by smoking.

Americans for Nonsmokers' Rights (ANR) was formed in

1976 in Berkeley, California. It has pushed through laws protecting nonsmokers in restaurants, public transportation, public places, and workplaces. ANR developed and maintains a National Resource Center to provide information on secondhand smoke, tobacco, and smokers' rights.

ANR also has a smoking prevention program called Teens as Teachers, which trains teens to teach children. The teens act as role models for the younger children. Teens go through training and develop their own presentations. They then visit lower grade classrooms when drug education is scheduled, and present their information, usually with small group activities.

Joseph Cherner heads SmokeFree Educational Services in New York City. This group promotes the right to live and work in a smoke-free world and educates young people about tobacco addiction. This group supports laws to: raise cigarette taxes, require all indoor public places to be smokefree, end free distribution of cigarettes, remove cigarette vending machines, end the use of tobacco products in public schools and on school property, and end tobacco company sponsoring of events for young people.

State and Local Governments

Many states, cities, and counties have passed laws to limit the availability and promotion of tobacco products to young people. Some of these laws include partial or total bans of tobacco vending machines and no tobacco sales to young people. If caught, businesses could lose their tobacco license and get fined. Bans on giving free tobacco product samples to young people are increasing. Although the tobacco industry has a code against giving free tobacco products to young people, many teens and children get free samples at public events, such as county fairs and festivals.

Five states—Maryland, California, Washington, Vermont, and Utah—have put restrictions on smoking into law. Over one hundred cities have smokefree restaurants. After the Environmental Protection Agency declared secondhand tobacco smoke a Group A carcinogen, hundreds of cities and several states have moved to ban smoking in public places. Maryland has passed the strictest ban so far on smoking in public and private workplaces in America.

California has been running an aggressive antismoking campaign for many years. The state uses a series of humorous TV ads and billboards to counter the tobacco industry advertising. Since the campaign started in 1990, cigarette sales in California have decreased by 1.1 billion packs or 27%. This is three times faster than elsewhere in the United States. The only group that has not decreased is teens.

In June 1993 the first tobacco victim case was heard in a small claims court. The Small Claims Court of Kings County, Washington, listened to a suit filed by Alan Deskiewicz. He had smoked for over thirty years and was suing a tobacco company to get back the money he had spent on trying to quit. This included doctor's bills and nicotine patches. The case was not continued due to expiration of the three-year limit on small claims cases. But, antismoking supporters plan to publish a how-to manual to help other ex-smokers who want to bring similar suits to small claims court.

People

People, acting alone or organized as groups, have taken many kinds of antitobacco and antismoking actions. Community groups can control billboards, as in the cities of Baltimore,

Maryland; Perth Amboy, New Jersey; Detroit, Michigan; and Philadelphia, Pennsylvania. In 1994 Baltimore banned tobacco advertising on billboards in most neighborhoods of the city. Community groups can also control sales to minors.

Ex-smokers with tobacco-related diseases have spoken up about their health problems from tobacco use. They hope their personal stories prevent others, especially young people, from using tobacco. They speak at schools and community events. Some well-known entertainers have talked honestly to the press, hoping to let others know the agony of their smoking-related diseases.

Multitalented entertainer, Sammy Davis, Jr., before his death at age sixty-four, told the real cause of his throat cancer: he had been a long-time, two-pack a day cigarette smoker. When asked about his cancer, he explained, "My throat was raw. If I touched it, my hand would come away with blood. I was losing weight. I couldn't eat. Everything tasted like mush."[12]

Recently, the New York newspapers carried the story of David Gorelitz. Gorelitz was a model for cigarette ads and smoked three packs a day for twenty-four years. He spoke to New York schoolchildren and apologized for his tobacco ads. He called cigarettes "the deadliest drug of all." He further explained, "The image I projected is nothing but a bunch of lies made up by ad executives and the tobacco industry."[13]

Health professionals also act as role models for teens. In early 1993 Bill Weigel, a pharmacist, stopped selling cigarettes at his drugstore in Golden Valley, Minnesota. He wanted to provide a positive influence. "Kids come into the pharmacy and see a health provider selling cigarettes, and might think that cigarettes are not so bad. If we can show them we care about their health or the diseases smoking causes, it is worth it."[14] By removing tobacco products, Bill Weigel also solved the problem of illegal sales to teens. The National Association of Boards of Pharmacy encourages pharmacy owners to remove tobacco products from their stores.

Another type of prevention was initiated by Janis Kent of Melrose, Massachusetts. As her young son watched a Walt Disney cartoon featuring a cowboy smoking a cigarette, she worried that he would "get the impression that this [smoking] is heroic behavior." So, she called the Walt Disney Production offices in Burbank, California, and complained. Disney called her back a few days later and said the cartoon had been taken off the air. Two weeks later, Disney again called to say that all their cartoons would be reviewed and edited to remove smoking scenes.[15]

Another type of prevention is countertactics. Neil Kuchinsky, an attorney in Virginia, created a public service announcement for strong tobacco control. In his television ad, he lashed out at one of the tobacco companies.

Questions For Discussion

1. What is your school's policy on tobacco use? Do you agree with it? If not, what should it be?

2. Physical activity, such as walking, jogging, or dancing, can produce a natural "high." Why?

3. Why do you think more adults than teens go to quit-smoking programs?

7

Smokeless Tobacco and Secondhand Smoke

Two serious teen problems that stand out today are smokeless tobacco and secondhand smoke, sometimes also known as environmental tobacco smoke or ETS. Both of these issues have received much attention on television and radio, in the newspapers, and in school programs.

What is Smokeless Tobacco?

People call smokeless tobacco by many names: chew, dip, pinch, snuff, plug, or dirt. There are really two basic kinds of smokeless tobacco. These are snuff (spit) and chewing tobacco. In the United States, most people use moist snuff. This is a tobacco product used by mouth. Users dip or tuck it between their lower lip and gum. Spit tobacco is made from whole tobacco leaves and added flavors, such as vanilla, licorice, or wintergreen.

Chewing tobacco is made from shredded leaves, sweeteners, and flavorings. The leaves are sold loose in packets, pressed into cakes (plugs), or twisted into strands. Users chew about an inch wad of the tobacco or hold it between the cheek and gum.

Alarming Increases in Spit Tobacco Use

By the 1970s the health risks of smoking became widely known. About this time, some users switched to spit tobacco. Why the switch? Since the mid-1970s, a large tobacco company has run huge advertising campaigns. Their ads have implied that spit tobacco is safer than cigarettes. Free samples were given to sports leagues and college teens. Famous athletes and entertainers were paid to appear in ads promoting smokeless tobacco. The tobacco company also sponsored many teen events.

The ads have been effective. The number of people, especially male teens, using spit tobacco has skyrocketed over the last two decades. Today the National Cancer Institute estimates that over twelve million Americans nationwide use smokeless tobacco regularly. Nearly two million of these people are teens, aged twelve to seventeen.[1] Nearly all of them are males. This means that one out of five high school males currently uses smokeless tobacco.[2] The Centers for Disease Control reports that Americans are using more chewing tobacco each year.

Many start young. National surveys show that the average starting age is between ten and twelve. Teens may begin using spit tobacco to copy an adult they look up to, like a coach, athlete, entertainer, or parent. The nicotine in the tobacco keeps them coming back for more. If parents or relatives use smokeless tobacco or approve of it, then teens are more likely to use it. "Guys chew because it's macho," said one high school senior. "Most guys in my class chew. On my football team of forty-five, only three of us didn't chew."[3]

Many teens and adults do not realize that smokeless tobacco ads do not tell the truth. Smokeless tobacco is unsafe, addictive, and costly.[4] One counselor admitted that he chews tobacco. But he said, "Few people know that I chew. It's a secret, because it's the worst addiction."[5]

Health Problems

In her December 1992 report, *Spit Tobacco and Youth*, Dr. Antonia Novello, former U.S. Surgeon General, warned, "I must tell you that there is no safe way to use tobacco. Tobacco is tobacco is tobacco. Spit tobacco [a synonym for smokeless tobacco] is dangerous to health—no matter whether it is spit, chewed, or swallowed."[6]

Oral Cancers

The International Agency for Research on Cancer, the World Health Organization, the National Institutes of Health, and Dr. Novello all agree: Smokeless tobacco causes oral cancer. Smokeless tobacco use, said Dr. Novello, poses a large health threat. "This threat is oral cancer—an epidemic in the making that will occur if young people continue to use 'spit' tobacco. I am deeply concerned by the attempts of the spit tobacco industry to downplay the health hazards posed by this type of tobacco."[7]

Statistics back up Dr. Novello's concerns. Each year the American Cancer Society reports 30,300 new cases of oral cancers. And, according to the American Cancer Society, half of these people—over fifteen thousand—will die within five years from the cancer. The executive vice president of the American Academy of Otolaryngology (Head and Neck Surgery) summed

Because many people do not realize the health dangers of smokeless tobacco, information like this pamphlet can help to inform current and potential users of possible health problems.

up what these statistics mean. "Smokeless tobacco users are trading lung cancer for oral cancer."[8]

Oral cancers can form quickly. Mouth sores are common among smokeless tobacco users, even among teens. After an average of just over three years, mouth sores can turn into cancer, according to studies by the American Academy of Otolaryngology.

Because of the high risk of developing oral cancer, the American Cancer Society recommends users check their mouth once a month for these five warning signs:

- A sore that bleeds easily and does not heal.
- A lump or thickening anywhere in the mouth.
- Soreness or swelling that will not go away.
- A red or white patch that will not go away.
- Trouble chewing, swallowing, or moving the tongue or jaw.

Heart Effects

Within five to thirty minutes of using smokeless tobacco, users can feel the effects. The nicotine in the tobacco makes the heart beat faster and increases blood pressure. Just as with the first-time cigarette users, first-time smokeless tobacco users usually feel dizzy, shaky, and nauseated, as nicotine enters the body.

Other Problems

Using smokeless tobacco can cause gum loss, tooth loss, loss of taste and smell, permanent tooth stains, and bad breath. The high sugar content of smokeless tobacco can also cause cavities.

In addition, users have to spit or swallow tobacco juices. They often find bits of tobacco between their teeth, gums, and cheeks.

Nicotine Addiction

The nicotine in smokeless tobacco can lead to addiction. Smokeless tobacco contains more nicotine than cigarettes. Researchers find that an average-sized dip or chew held in the mouth for thirty minutes, releases as much nicotine as smoking four cigarettes. If someone uses two cans of spit tobacco in one week, or smokes one-and-a-half packs of cigarettes a day, the amount of nicotine received is the same. And, just like cigarettes, some brands of smokeless tobacco deliver more nicotine than others.

NICOTINE ADDICTION	
Stages	**Signs of Addiction**
Early	Users no longer get sick or dizzy when they use dip or chew.
	Users dip or chew more often and in more different situations. They often switch to smokeless tobacco with more nicotine.
Hard-core	Users must dip or chew early in the day, often before breakfast.
	Users need to dip or chew every few hours.
	If users try to quit, they have strong cravings for smokeless tobacco.

The National Cancer Institute divides nicotine addiction from smokeless tobacco into two stages: early and hard-core.

Prevention

The federal government has taken only a few steps to slow the use of smokeless tobacco. In 1986 the Comprehensive Smokeless Tobacco Health Education Act passed. Because of this law, at least one of the following health warnings is required on all smokeless tobacco products:

- Warning: This Product May Cause Mouth Cancer
- Warning: This Product May Cause Gum Disease and Tooth Loss
- Warning: This Product Is Not a Safe Alternative to Cigarettes

There are also bans on all radio and television ads for smokeless tobacco. However, according to the national organization Stop Teenage Addiction to Tobacco (STAT), these bans have not impacted sales much. The tobacco companies have found other ways to reach teens. A large chunk of tobacco companies' advertising budgets goes toward free samples and sponsoring events.

Some state governments, such as Washington and Maine, tax smokeless products heavily. Price is one way to get teens to quit. "The only reason kids kick the chewing habit is because of cost. It typically runs $20 a week," stated eighteen-year-old Jake Trippel.[9]

As of 1993, California and some cities across the United States have banned free samples of smokeless products. However, like cigarettes, smokeless tobacco is available in many stores. Nationwide studies find that most stores sell smokeless tobacco to teens. Also, many schools do not ban smokeless tobacco use by students or staff.

Baseball organizations are responding. In 1990, Major League Baseball issued a report on the hazards of smokeless tobacco. In minor league baseball and on some major league teams, chew tobacco is banned. Many baseball players have stopped using smokeless tobacco and instead chew gum or sunflower seeds. Each spring over six hundred thousand ballplayers ages six to eighteen in the Babe Ruth League learn about the health risks of smokeless tobacco.

Secondhand Smoke

Secondhand smoke is the smoke exhaled by smokers, mixed with the smoke that comes from burning tobacco. It is also called passive, involuntary, or environmental tobacco smoke (ETS). Anyone exposed to secondhand smoke breathes in over four thousand chemical substances. Many of these substances are poisons: tar, nicotine, carbon monoxide, arsenic, and cyanide are just of few of the possibilities.

A recent report from the Centers for Disease Control stated that secondhand smoke kills 53,000 Americans each year. It is the third largest preventable cause of death.[10] Only direct smoking and alcohol-related deaths rank higher.[11] According to the National Cancer Institute, each year secondhand smoke causes about three thousand lung cancer deaths in nonsmokers.

Health Hazards

In addition to causing cancer in people, secondhand smoke increases the risk of developing heart disease and asthma.

The National Center for Health Statistics estimates that

Is YOUR BABY SMOKING?

IF SOMEONE IN YOUR HOUSEHOLD IS SMOKING, THEN YOUR BABY IS SMOKING, TOO.

Critics say that smoking while pregnant or with children or teens in the house is the same as child abuse.

children who live with a smoker are almost twice as likely to be in poor health compared with children who come from nonsmoking homes. The more a child or teen is exposed to secondhand smoke, the greater the harm. The greatest amount of damage occurs in infants under the age of two. Their lungs are still developing and they have less ability to fight diseases.

Breathing secondhand smoke can cause respiratory problems for nonsmokers such as coughing and wheezing. Headaches, nausea, and watery, itchy, red eyes are also common. Each year nearly three hundred thousand infections such as colds, flu, bronchitis, and pneumonia in babies and infants are due to breathing secondhand smoke. Breathing in secondhand smoke can also cause fluid backups in the middle ear. This can lead to ear infections. Sudden Infant Death Syndrome (SIDS) occurs two-and-a-half times more frequently among babies whose mothers smoke. Everyone is harmed by tobacco smoke, even unborn children and infants. There is no safe level of exposure to tobacco smoke.

Young People's Rights

As the evidence about the effects of secondhand smoke grows, the courts are granting nonsmokers more rights. This is especially true if young people are involved. For example, in custody and divorce cases, courts have ruled that parents cannot smoke around their children. In October 1993, Susan Tanner, a smoker, lost custody of her eight-year-old daughter. The father, a nonsmoker, had taken his asthmatic daughter to a doctor because of her wheezing. The girl had a high level of nicotine in her blood in addition to reduced breathing ability.

In another case, Joseph Lamacchia got a court order to

prohibit his ex-wife or anyone else from smoking around his young son. After his victory in 1992, Lamacchia co-founded Parents Against Secondhand Smoke (PASS). It is based in Watertown, Massachusetts. It offers counseling to parents involved in divorces or custody cases where secondhand smoke is a factor.

Workplaces

Some secondhand smoke victims have recently begun to sue their employers. One example is a woman in Los Angeles, California. She sued her former employer because she became sick from secondhand smoke on the job. She had repeatedly asked for a smoke-free workplace, but was ignored.

In March 1994, thirty former flight attendants of various airlines sued the major cigarette makers. The case before the Florida State Court is the first to try to show that these people got sick as a direct result of secondhand smoke.

Secondhand smoke in restaurants is also under attack. According to a study by Dr. Michael Siegel at the Centers for Disease Control, waiters and bartenders are at a 50 percent higher risk of developing lung cancer. "Everyone talks about the risks of secondhand smoke for restaurant customers. But restaurant workers face an even greater risk."[12]

Workers who suffer health problems because they work in restaurants are suing restaurant owners. One recent case occurred in California. A waiter had a heart attack while working in a smoke-filled bar. The waiter sued the restaurant and won.

Fast-food restaurants are also a concern. "Because fast-food restaurants successfully market to children and because teenagers make up a large segment of the fast food workforce, these restaurants have a special obligation to eliminate tobacco smoke," said New York Attorney General Bob Abrams.[13] John Banzhaf, executive director of Action on Smoking and Health (ASH) agrees. He has warned fast-food chains that they could be sued if a child has an asthma attack in their restaurant.

Increasing Smoking Restrictions

Since the 1980s acceptance of smoking around nonsmokers has been steadily declining. Today nonsmokers demand clean, smoke-free public places and workplaces. Pollution control has become a major issue. Peter F. Vallone, Speaker for the New York City Council, explained, "A nonsmoker has to be provided with a smoke-free environment. This is not a rights issue. It is a public health issue."[14]

More and more smoking restrictions are in effect today:

- Most American hospitals are smoke-free.

- The federal government restricts smoking in all of its buildings. All forty thousand United States Postal Services facilities are smoke-free.

- The District of Columbia and many other states ban smoking in public places.

- All regularly scheduled buses and 99 percent of air flights within the United States are smoke-free. Many airports in the United States ban smoking.

- Amtrak estimates that over 80 percent of its trains are now smoke-free.

- Most hotels and motels in the United States have smoke-free rooms.

- Many colleges and universities across the United States have banned all tobacco use.

- The National Collegiate Athletic Association (NCAA) bans all tobacco use during practices and games.
- Minor league baseball teams ban all tobacco use. Major league baseball teams offer smoke-free seating in most stadiums.
- About two-thirds of American businesses are smoke-free.[15]
- Many fast-food restaurants are now smoke-free or are experimenting with a smoking ban.
- Cities across the United States are passing tougher laws. For example, Brookline, Massachusetts, passed a law in 1994 that bans cigarette vending machines. It also requires all restaurants, hotels, motels, taxis, public places, and workplaces to be smoke-free. New York City, New York; Los Angeles, California; Aspen, Colorado; and Madison, Wisconsin, have also passed tough antimoking laws.

Questions For Discussion

1. Why do you think the government bans radio and television ads for spit tobacco?

2. How do you think ads could be written to discourage people from using spit tobacco?

3. Would you refuse to sell cigarettes to a pregnant woman? Why or why not?

4. What can you do to protect yourself from secondhand smoke?

8

Where Are We Today?

America's policies toward smoking are changing quickly today. All types of government—federal, state, and local—are establishing more aggressive controls. Great effort is now focused on stopping illegal sales of cigarettes to young people. Prices are being raised. And, advertising and promotion of tobacco products is being restricted. With the emphasis on clean air in the United States, secondhand smoke is increasingly being banned from public areas and workplaces. The federal government is taking a stronger role in proposing laws that regulate tobacco products and secondhand smoke.

Federal Actions

In the 103rd Congress of the United States, many bills dealing with tobacco and health have been introduced. Support is growing for the Smoke-Free Environment Act. This would require that all enclosed buildings be smoke-free if more than ten people enter the building each week. This means that most public places would be smoke-free. The federal government voted to increase their tax on each pack of cigarettes by $1.25. More than a hundred tobacco control and health groups want a $2.00 increase, but President Clinton suggested a seventy-five cent increase. The higher the cost of cigarettes, the less people smoke. The American Cancer Society estimates that a $2.00 a pack tax increase would save almost two million lives.

ABC News, after a year of investigation into the tobacco industry, aired a television show on February 28, 1994. They claimed that the tobacco industry changes the nicotine levels in cigarettes. The higher amounts of nicotine hook new users and keep current smokers addicted. If the tobacco industry is controlling the nicotine in cigarettes and selling cigarettes to satisfy an addiction, then the FDA can regulate cigarettes as a drug. Based on the information provided by ABC News, the FDA is seeking advice on how to regulate cigarettes. The FDA has called for a hearing and is now gathering information from seven major American tobacco companies.

On March 23, 1994, Congress proposed an amendment to outlaw smoking in most American schools. The only exceptions would be for areas that are closed off to young people, with outside ventilation. The ban would cover most public and some private schools.

The Occupational Safety and Health Administration (OSHA) proposed a rule on March 26, 1994, that would ban smoking in the workplace. Seventy million Americans, including large numbers of teens, work indoors. About twenty-one million of them are exposed to poor indoor air, including secondhand smoke. Before the rule can become final, thousands of comments must be reviewed, including comments from the general public.

In 1984 Congress passed the law requiring the warning labels that are still used on cigarette packs. The Federal Trade Commission also wants to require warning labels on racing cars which carry smokeless tobacco ads.

State and City Actions

The city of New York has proposed a strong smoke-free law. It is called "The Smoke-Free Air Act." This would make most public places and workplaces smoke-free. This would include restaurants, playgrounds, child-care facilities, outdoor concerts with assigned seating, and outdoor sports arenas. New York City has been a national leader in clean indoor air laws since 1987. Since then, it has done away with free samples of cigarettes, most cigarette vending machines, tobacco use on school property, and tobacco ads on many means of public transportation. The city is currently holding hearings on "The Smoke-Free Air Act."

Since 1990, California also has been a national leader in the fight against smoking. The state is using taxes and ad campaigns to reduce cigarette use. It has succeeded by nearly 30 percent. However, the largest tobacco company in the country was able to get a proposal in favor of smoking on the public election ballot for November of 1994. Business and building owners, not the state government, would decide where to allow smoking. This is the first time the cigarette industry has taken a pro-smoking proposal to the voters in a state.

So far, California's five-year success in controlling tobacco is still a national model. Tobacco use in California is down by 30 percent. Arizona, Arkansas, Colorado, Massachusetts, Oregon, and Virginia are looking closely at ways to follow the California program. In July 1994, the state of Maryland put into law the toughest antismoking policy in the nation up to that date.

In a first case of its kind, Mississippi is demanding that the cigarette companies pay the health care cost of smoking. The state is suing the tobacco industry for the costs of medical programs that support people with smoking-related illnesses. The suit is unusual because it is the first time a government has said that the tobacco companies are responsible for the health consequences of their products. Other states are following this case with great interest. Florida may be the next state to follow with a similar case.

Looking Toward Tomorrow

Over seventy-five national pro health organizations support current federal and state policies for tougher laws against smoking. Their goal is to stop tobacco use and nicotine addiction. They hope to make America smoke-free by the year 2000. Whether this, or some other variation of restrictions will be put into place remains to be seen. Ultimately, the decision not to start smoking, or to quit smoking is entirely up to you.

Chapter Notes

Chapter 1

1. Mattoon Curtis, *Snuff and Snuff Boxes* (New York: Liverwright Publishing Corporation, 1935), p. 19.

2. Ibid., pp. 28–29.

3. Ibid., p. 31.

4. David Armstrong and Elizabeth Armstrong, *The Great American Medicine Show* (New York: Prentice Hall, 1991), p. 15.

5. Curtis, p. 77.

6. The Tobacco Institute, *Tobacco: Deeply Rooted in America's Heritage*, booklet (Washington, D.C.: The Tobacco Institute, n.d.), p. 5.

7. Cassandra Tate, "Still Smoking," *Smithsonian Magazine*, July 1989, p. 111.

8. C. Barr Taylor, et. al., *The Facts about Smoking* (New York: Consumer Reports Books, 1991), p. 6.

9. Tate, p. 112.

10. Ronald J. Troyer, *The Battle over Smoking* (New Brunswick, N.J.: Rutgers University Press, 1983), pp. 33–34.

11. The Tobacco Institute, p. 6.

12. U.S. Bureau of Alcohol, Tobacco, and Firearms, *An Introduction to the Bureau of Alcohol, Tobacco, and Firearms and the Regulated Industries,* (Washington, D.C.: U.S. Government Printing Office, March 1990), p. 2.

13. USDA—Economic Research Service, *Tobacco: Situation and Outlook*, April 1994.

Chapter 2

1. Personal correspondence from Dr. John Slade, Associate Professor, University of Medicine and Dentistry, N.J., May 24, 1994.

2. The Tobacco Institute, *Tobacco Industry Profile 1993*, pamphlet (Washington, D.C.: The Tobacco Institute, 1994), p. 1.

3. "Can China Kick the Habit?" on *NOVA*, television show that aired on the public education channel, April 12, 1994.

4. Philip Cohen, *Tobacco* (Austin, Tex.: Steck-Vaughn Library, 1992), p. 17.

5. Centers for Disease Control and Prevention, "Mortality Trends for Selected Smoking-Related Cancers and Breast Cancer—United States, 1950–1990," *MMWE: Morbidity and Mortality Weekly Report*, November 12, 1993, p. 857.

6. "Tobacco Smoke Contains Radioactive Material," *SmokeFree Air* (Winter 1993–1994), p. 7.

7. Minnesota Prevention Resource Center, *Questions about Tobacco*, pamphlet (Anoka, Minn.: Minnesota Prevention Resource Center, 1990), p. 1.

8. Ibid., p. 2.

9. C. B. Taylor, *The Facts about Smoking* (New York: Consumer Reports Books, 1991), p. 75.

10. Smoking Education Program, *Nurses: Help Your Patients Stop Smoking*, booklet (Bethesda, Md.: National Heart, Lung, and Blood Institute, National Institutes of Health, 1993), p. 4.

11. Smoking Education Program, *Clinical Opportunities for Smoking Intervention: A Guide for the Busy Physician*, booklet (Bethesda, Md.: National Heart, Lung, and Blood Institute, National Institutes of Health, 1992), p. 13.

12. "Cancer Deaths," *Nutrition Act*, May 1993, p. 2.

13. Marion Merrell Dow, Inc., *The Economic Impact of Smoking on Dental and Oral Health*, booklet (Kansas City, Mo.: Marion Merrell Dow, Inc., December, 1991), p. 6.

14. "Smokers with HIV Get AIDS More Rapidly, Researchers Find," *Baltimore Sun*, May 12, 1993, p. 11A.

15. Joe Tye, "Protecting Babies from Philip Morris & RJR Nabisco," *Tobacco-Free Youth Reporter*, Spring 1993, p. 6.

16. "Secondhand Tobacco Smoke: How Dangerous Is It?" *Mayo Clinic Health Letter*, newsletter, June 1993, p. 7.

17. Office for Substance Abuse Prevention, "Hazards of Prenatal Exposure to Alcohol, Tobacco, and Other Drugs," *Alcohol, Tobacco, and Other Drugs May Harm the Unborn*, booklet (Rockville, Md.: Alcohol, Drug Abuse, and Mental Health Administration, reprinted 1992), p. 23.

18. Teres Carr, "Smoking and Breast Milk," *American Health*, April 1994, p. 110.

19. "Smoke Gets in Your Eyes," *Monday Morning Reports*, newsletter, January 25, 1993, p. 3.

Chapter 3

1. Suzann Stenso-Velo, "Cowboy 'Snuffs' 200,000 Each Year," *Minnesota Department of Health ASSIST Quarterly*, newsletter, October 1993, p. 1.

2. Ibid.

3. "What Teens Spend on Tobacco," *Tobacco-Free Youth Reporter*, Spring 1994, p. 1.

4. Americans for Nonsmokers' Rights, *Youth and Tobacco*, fact sheet (Berkeley, Calif.: Americans for Nonsmokers' Rights, 1993).

5. Author interview with Jake Trippel, White Bear Lake, Minn., May 17, 1993.

6. "Teen Smokers Find Quitting Tougher Than They Think," *The Nation's Health*, January 1993, p. 10.

7. Americans for Nonsmokers' Rights, "Youth Access to Tobacco," (Berkeley, Calif.: Americans for Nonsmokers' Rights, 1992), p. 1.

8. Karen Casey, *If Only I Could Quit: Becoming a Nonsmoker,* (New York: Harper & Row, 1987), p. 48.

9. Betty Gibb, *Tobacco: Smoking or the Glamorous Life*, booklet (Silver Spring, Md.: The Health Connection, 1990), p. 1.

10. Author interview with Jake Trippel, White Bear Lake, Minn., May 17, 1993.

11. The American College of Obstetricians and Gynecologists, *Smoking and Women*, pamphlet (Washington, D.C.: The American College of Obstetricians and Gynecologists, 1991), p. 1.

12. Robert Robinson, *Pathways to Freedom: Winning the Fight Against Tobacco*, booklet (Philadelphia: Fox Chase Cancer Center, 1992), p. 4.

13. American Lung Association, *Facts about Cigarette Smoking*, pamphlet (New York: American Lung Association, 1990), p. 3.

14. "U.S. Smoking Related Deaths Decline Slightly—Worldwide Explosion Expected," *Tobacco-Free Youth Reporter*, Autumn 1993, p. 18.

15. "Cigarette Smoking Losing Favor Around the World," *The Bottom Line on Alcohol in Society*, Winter 1992, p. 78.

16. Masumi Minowa and Hiroshi Satomi, "Japan: Sales of Tobacco to Minors," *The Lancet*, May 9, 1992, p. 1,163.

17. Office on Smoking and Health, *Smoking and Health in the Americas: A 1992 Report of the Surgeon General in Collaboration with the Pan American Health Organization*, pamphlet (Atlanta: National Center for Chronic Disease Prevention and Health Promotion, U.S. Department of Health and Human Services, 1992), p. 2.

18. Suzann Stenso-Velo, "Cowboy 'Snuffs' 200,000 Each Year," *Minnesota Department of Health ASSIST Quarterly*, newsletter, October 1993, p. 1.

19. "Advertising Linked to Increased Youth Smoking," *Tobacco-Free Youth Reporter*, Spring 1994, p. 14.

20. Author telephone interview with Diane Benjamin, ASSIST Field Director, Community Action for a Tobacco-Free Environment, Minnesota Department of Health, January 24, 1994.

21. Nicole Carroll, "Surgeon General's Warning: Tobacco Firms Target Kids," *USA Today*, February 24, 1994, p. 1A.

Chapter 4

1. Wolfgang Schivelbusch, *Tastes of Paradise: A Social History of Spices, Stimulants, and Intoxicants* (New York: Vintage Books, 1992), p. 130.

2. Kevin R. Cooper, "From King to Culprit: Tobacco," *Virginia Medical*, August 1986, p. 459.

3. Schivelbush, p. 120.

4. William Ecenbarger, "The Strange History of Tobacco," *Readers Digest*, April 1992, p. 141.

5. Center for Disease Control and Prevention, "Mortality Trends for Selected Smoking-Related Cancers and Breast Cancer—United States, 1950–1990," *MMWE: Morbidity and Mortality Weekly Report*, November 12, 1993, p. 857.

6. Smoking Education Program, *Nurses: Help Your Patients Stop Smoking*, booklet (Bethesda, Md.: National Heart, Lung, and Blood Institute, National Institutes of Health, 1993), p. 4.

7. American Lung Association, *Facts about Cigarette Smoking*, pamphlet (White Plains, N.Y.: American Lung Association, November 1990).

8. Marion Merrell Dow, Inc., *The Economic Impact of Smoking on Pulmonary Health*, booklet (Kansas City, Mo.: Marion Merrell Dow, Inc., December 1991), p. 4.

9. Author telephone interview with Stan Stuart, Director of National Fire Data Center, United States Fire Administration, Emmitsburg, Md., February 4, 1994.

10. "Cigarettes Could Be Less of a Fire Hazard," *Tobacco-Free Youth Reporter*, Spring 1994, pp. 14, 19.

11. The Wisconsin Clearinghouse, Mood-Altering Chemicals, booklet (Madison, Wis.: The Wisconsin Clearinghouse, 1987), p. 53.

Chapter 5

1. A. C. Heath and N. G. Martin, "Genetic Models for the Natural History of Smoking: Evidence for a Genetic Influence on Smoking Persistence," *Addictive Behavior*, Vol. 18, 1993, pp. 31–32.

2. Karen Casey, *If Only I Could Quit: Becoming a Nonsmoker* (New York: Harper & Row, 1987), pp. 7–8.

3. Life Skills Education, *Smoking & Your Kids*, booklet (Northfield, Minn: Life Skills Education, 1992), p. 3.

4. Ibid., pp. 2–3.

5. Ovide Pomerleau, "Behavioral Factors in the Establishment, Maintenance, and Cessation of Smoking," *The Behavioral Aspects of Smoking* (National Institute on Drug Abuse Research Monograph 26, U.S. Department of Health, Education, and Welfare, 1979), p. 50.

6. Life Skills Education, *What Is Addiction: Who Is an Addict?* booklet (Northfield, Minn.: Life Skills Education, 1991), p. 12.

7. Smoking Education Program, *How You Can Help Patients Stop Smoking*, booklet (Bethesda, Md.: National Heart, Lung, and Blood Institute, National Institutes of Health, 1991), p. 18.

8. Life Skills Education, *Smoking & Your Kids*, p. 11.

9. "Self-exempting Beliefs," *University of California at Berkeley Wellness Letter*, newsletter, August 1993, p. 7.

Chapter 6

1. National Cancer Institute, *Clearing the Air: How to Quit Smoking . . . and Quit for Keeps*, booklet (Rockville, Md.: National Institutes of Health, U.S. Department of Health and Human Services, 1992), p. 3.

2. Andrew Tobias, *Kids Say Don't Smoke* (New York: Workman Publishing, 1991), p. 58.

3. Centers for Disease Control, *The Health Benefits of Smoking Cessation: A Report of the Surgeon General, 1990*, pamphlet (Atlanta: Office on Smoking and Health, National Center for Chronic Disease Prevention and Health Promotion, 1990), p. 3.

4. United States Department of Education, *What Works, Schools Without Drugs*, booklet (Washington, D.C.: U.S. Department of Education, 1992), p. 61.

5. Author interview with Jake Trippel, White Bear Lake, Minn., May 15, 1993.

6. Betty Gibb, *Tobacco: Smoking or the Glamorous Life*, pamphlet (Silver Spring, Md.: The Health Connection, 1990), p. 5.

7. Author interviews with Pam Solstad, "Freedom from Smoking" facilitator for the American Lung Association, St. Paul, Minn., September 16 and 28, 1993.

8. John Newport, "Best Way to Quit Smoking," *Readers Digest*, December 1993, p. 105.

9. Author interviews with Pam Solstad.

10. Ibid., September 28, 1993.

11. "Query about positive influences prompts many student opinions," *On TARGET*, May 1993, p. 5.

12. Andrew Tobias, *Kids Say Don't Smoke* (New York: Workman Publishing, 1991), p. 46.

13. "Wayne McLaren, Marlboro Man, Dies of Lung Cancer," *Tobacco-Free Youth Reporter*, Fall 1992, p. 23.

14. Judy Knapp, "Local Pharmacy Phases Out Cigarettes," *Countdown: Newsletter of the Minnesota Coalition for a Smoke-Free Society 2000*, newsletter, Spring 1993, pp. 1, 6.

15. Janis Kent, "One Person Does Make a Difference," *Minnesota Department of Health Quarterly ASSIST*, newsletter, August 1993, p. 3.

Chapter 7

1. National Cancer Institute, *Chew or Snuff is Real Bad Stuff: A Guide to Make Young People Aware of the Dangers of Using Smokeless Tobacco*, booklet (Bethesda, Md.: National Institutes of Health, U.S. Department of Health and Human Services, 1993), p. 2.

2. "Inspector General Warns of Dangers of Spit Tobacco," *Tobacco-Free Youth Reporter*, Spring 1993, p. 20.

3. Author interview with Jake Trippel, White Bear Lake, Minn., May 17, 1993.

4. National Cancer Institute, *Chew or Snuff is Real Bad Stuff*, p. 2.

5. Author interview with anonymous source, St. Paul, Minn., June 8, 1993.

6. "Spit Tobacco: A National Epidemic," *Tobacco-Free Youth Reporter*, Spring 1993, p. 21.

7. Ibid., p.7.

8. Kevin Waite, *Smokeless Tobacco: Three Strikes, You're Out*, booklet (Hagerstown, Md.: The Health Connection, 1992), pp. 3–4.

9. Author interview with Jake Trippel, White Bear Lake, Minn., June 17, 1993.

10. Thomas Houston, "The Silent Killer: Environmental Tobacco Smoke," *The Journal of Family Practice*, October 1990, p. 457.

11. Eva Rumpf, "Secondhand Smoke Puts You at Risk," *Current Health 2*, November 1992, p. 20.

12. "Restaurant Smoking Sickens Waiters," *SmokeFree Air*, newsletter, Winter 1993–1994, p. 3.

13. "Attorney Generals Call for Smoke-Free Fast Food," *SmokeFree Air*, newsletter, Winter 1993–1994, p. 3.

14. "Believe or Not" *SmokeFree Air*, newsletter, Fall 1993, p. 6.

15. "New York City Proposes Strong Smoke-Free Law," *SmokeFree Air*, newsletter, Summer 1994, p. 1.

Chapter 8

No notes

Where To Go For Help

Quit-Smoking Programs

American Cancer Society
1599 Clifton Road NE
Atlanta, GA 30329
(800) 227-2345

American Lung Association
1740 Broadway
New York, NY 10019
(800) LUNG-USA

American Heart Association
7272 Greenville Avenue
Dallas, TX 75231
(214) 373-6300
Or, look in your telephone
directory for a local branch.

National Cancer Institute
900 Rockville Pike
Bethesda, MD 20892
(800)-4-CANCER
"Clearing the Air"

Self-Help Materials

American Cancer Society
1599 Clifton Road NE
Atlanta, GA 30329
(800) 227-2345
Booklets and pamphlets on how to quit smoking

National Cancer Institute
9000 Rockville Pike
Bethesda, MD 20892
(800) 4-CANCER
Information about how to stop smoking and using smokeless tobacco

Hazelden
15251 Pleasant Valley Road
P.O. Box 176
Center City, MN 55102-0176
(800) 328-9000
Quit-smoking books, booklets, pamphlets

Office on Smoking and Health
Centers for Chronic Disease
Prevention and Health Promotion
Mail Stop K-50
1600 Clifton Road NE
Atlanta, GA 30333
(404) 488-5705
Books and pamphlets on how to quit smoking and using smokeless tobacco

The Health Connection
55 West Oak Ridge Drive
Hagerstown, MD 21740
(800) 548-8700
Information for teens on how to quit

American Cancer Society
1599 Clifton Road NE
Atlanta, GA 30329
(800) 227-2345
Information about tobacco-related cancers; quit-smoking programs

American Dental Association
211 East Chicago Avenue
Chicago, IL 60611-2678
(312) 440-2500
Information about tobacco-related oral cancers and smokeless tobacco

American Lung Association
1740 Broadway
New York, NY 10019
(800)LUNG-USA
Information about tobacco-related lung diseases and smoking and pregnancy; quit-smoking programs

Americans for NonSmokers' Rights Foundation
2530 San Pablo Avenue
Berkeley, CA 94702-2013
(510) 841-3032
Smoking and health information; information on laws about smoking; publishes newsletter; runs a youth smoking prevention program called "Teens as Teachers."

American Heart Association
7272 Greenville Avenue
Dallas, TX 75231
(214) 373-6300
Information about tobacco-related heart disease and stroke; quit-smoking programs

Bureau of Alcohol, Tobacco, and Firearms
650 Massachusetts Avenue NW
Washington, DC 20226
(202) 927-7777
Information on tobacco taxes, labeling, import, export

Coalition on Smoking or Health
Suite 820
1150 Connecticut Avenue NW
Washington, DC 20036
(202) 452-1184
Information on laws on smoking and health

Environmental Protection Agency (EPA)
Public Information
Waterside West Building
401 M Street SW
Washington, DC 20460
(202) 260-2080
Information on control of pollution by air and water and by toxic substances such as tobacco smoke

The Health Connection
55 West Oak Ridge Drive
Hagerstown, MD 21740
(800) 548-8700
Information for teens on smoking and health and appearance; smokeless tobacco; how to stop smoking

March of Dimes Birth Defects Foundation
1275 Mamaroneck Avenue
White Plains, NY 10605
(914) 428-7100
Information about smoking and pregnancy; how parental smoking affects children

National Cancer Institute
9000 Rockville Pike
Bethesda, MD 20892
(800) 4-CANCER
Information about tobacco-related cancers and how to stop using tobacco

National Heart, Lung, and Blood Institute
9000 Rockville Pike
Bethesda, MD 20892
(301) 251-1222
Information about tobacco-related heart and lung diseases

Office on Smoking and Health
Public Information Branch
Centers for Chronic Disease Prevention and Health Promotion
Mail Stop K-50
1600 Clifton Road NE
Atlanta, GA 30333
(404) 488-5705
Information on smoking and health, tobacco-related diseases, how to quit smoking and using smokeless tobacco, and what is in tobacco smoke

Smokefree Educational Services
275 South End Avenue
Suite 32F
New York, NY 10280
(212) 912-0960
Publishes newsletter and other materials about smoke-free rights, laws, and education of teens about tobacco addiction

Stop Teenage Addiction to Tobacco (STAT)
511 E. Columbus Avenue
Springfield, MA 01105
(413) 732-7828
Information on preventing teen addiction to tobacco; publishes Tobacco-Free Youth Reporter (newspaper)

Glossary

Acquired Immunodeficiency Syndrome (AIDS)—A deadly viral disease that destroys the ability of the body's immune system to protect itself.

addict—Someone who is dependent on or controlled by a drug.

air sacs—Tiny pouches that line the surface of the lungs and move oxygen from the lungs into the bloodstream.

arteriosclerosis—Narrowing of the arteries by buildup of fatty materials such as cholesterol on the artery walls. Over time, the artery walls thicken and harden. Blood flow slows, so less oxygen travels to body tissues. This can lead to shortness of breath or death from heart attacks or strokes.

bronchitis—A lung disease that causes coughing and shortness of breath.

carbon monoxide—A highly poisonous, odorless gas that is given off in tobacco smoke.

carcinogen—A substance that causes cancer.

cataracts—Clouding of the eye lens which can lead to partial or total blindness.

chewing tobacco—Twisted or loose-leaf tobacco sold in plugs, bricks, or pouches. A wad of chewing tobacco is held between the cheek and gum and chewed.

Chronic Obstructive Lung Disease (COPD)—Chronic bronchitis and emphysema. Smokers can have both diseases at the same time.

cilia—Tiny hairlike structures that project from the surface of the lungs' air sacs. Cilia sweep out dirt, bacteria, and other foreign material from the lungs.

dip—Finely cut, ground, or powdered tobacco that is sold in both dry and moist forms. Moist dip or snuff is most commonly used by teens. A pinch or dip is packed between the cheek and gum, or lower lip and gum, and kept there.

emphysema—A lung disease which destroys the lungs' elasticity so they cannot inhale and exhale normally.

fetus—An unborn, developing baby.

genetics—A branch of biology dealing with heredity.

human immunodeficiency virus (HIV)—The virus that causes AIDS.

immunity—The body's ability to fight diseases.

miscarriage—The death of the fetus and its expulsion from the mother's uterus.

mucus—A sticky, slippery liquid material secreted by the lungs as a protective, lubricating coating.

nicotine—An addictive drug contained in tobacco.

nicotine gum—Gum containing small amounts of nicotine that is used by people who are trying to quit smoking. People stop smoking and instead chew ten to fifteen pieces of gum each day. Over time, people chew less and less gum.

nicotine patch—Nicotine patches help people quit smoking. The nicotine inside the gel slowly passes through the skin and into the bloodstream. Twenty-four hours later, when all the nicotine is gone, smokers remove the patch and put on a new one.

oral cancer—Cancers of the mouth, lip, tongue, larynx (voice box), and esophagus (swallowing tube).

osteoporosis—An inability by the body to absorb calcium, causing bones to become brittle, fragile, and weakened.

phlegm—Thick mucus.

premature—Born before thirty-seven weeks.

prescription—A doctor's orders or instructions for a drug.

relapse—Using tobacco again after a period of not using tobacco.

secondhand smoke—The smoke exhaled by smokers mixed with the smoke that comes from burning tobacco. It is also called passive, involuntary, or environmental tobacco smoke.

snuff—Finely cut tobacco. It is also called dip or smokeless tobacco. Sometimes snuff is drawn up into the nostrils by inhaling.

spit (smokeless) tobacco—Dip or snuff and chewing tobacco. Dip, made from finely cut tobacco leaves, is held between the lower lip and gum; it is not chewed. Chewing tobacco is chewed or held between the gum and cheek.

stillbirth—A baby who at birth shows no signs of life.

Sudden Infant Death Syndrome (SIDS)—The sudden, unexpected death of any infant or young child; the cause of death is unknown.

tar—A thick, oily, dark mixture that forms on the lungs when tobacco is smoked. Tar causes cancer.

tobacco—A plant grown for its large leaves which are made into cigarettes, pipe tobacco, cigars, snuff, or chew.

tolerance—The process by which a body becomes used to a drug so that the drug no longer has an effect. An increased drug dose is then needed to get the same effect of a lower dose.

withdrawal—The process of ridding the body of nicotine.

Further Reading

Books For Teen Readers

Berger, Gilda. "Tobacco" in *Addiction*. New York: Franklin Watts, 1992.

Cohen, Philip. *Tobacco*. Austin, Tex.: Steck-Vaughn Library, 1992.

Gano, Lila. *Smoking. San Diego, Calif.: Lucent Books, 1989.*

Keyishian, Elizabeth. *Everything You Need to Know about Smoking.* New York: Rosen Publishing Group, 1989.

Sonnett, Sherry. *Smoking.* New York: Franklin Watts, 1988.

Stepney, Rob. *Tobacco.* New York: Franklin Watts, 1987.

Tobias, Andrew. *Kids Say Don't Smoke.* New York: Workman Publishing, 1991.

Other Books

Casey, Karen. *If Only I Could Quit: Becoming a Nonsmoker.* New York: Harper & Row, 1987.

Galloway, Arlene. *The Smoke-Free Guide.* Victoria B.C.: Quaky Pub., 1988.

Krogh, David. *Smoking: the Artificial Passion.* New York: W.H. Freeman, 1991.

Orleans, C. Tracy and John Slade, eds. *Nicotine Addiction: Principles and Management.* New York: Oxford University Press, 1993.

1994 Surgeon General Report: Report on Smoking and Health.

Taylor, Barry C. *The Facts about Smoking.* New York: Consumer Reports Books, 1991.

Troyer, Ronald and Gerald Markle. *The Battle over Smoking.* New Brunswick, N.J.: Rutgers University Press, 1983.

White, Larry. *Merchants of Death: The American Tobacco Industry.* New York: Beech Tree Books, William Morrow, 1988.

Index